Practice Papers for SQA Exams

National 5

English

ISBN 9780007504879

Published by
Leckie & Leckie Ltd
An imprint of HarperCollinsPublishers
Westerhill Road, Bishopbriggs, Glasgow, G64 2QT
T: 0844 576 8126 F: 0844 576 8131
leckieandleckie@harpercollins.co.uk
www.leckieandleckie.co.uk

Special thanks to
Anna Penman (copy-edit); Jill Laidlaw (proofread);
Donna Cole (proofread); Rona Gloag (project management)
QBS (layout); Ink Tank (cover design)

A CIP Catalogue record for this book is available from the British Library.

Printed in Italy by Grafica Veneta S.p.A.

Acknowledgements
Extract from *What sport tells us about life* by Ed Smith (pages 9–10) was reproduced by permission of Penguin Books Ltd; extract from 'Can an ape learn to be human?' by Steve Connor (pages 46–47), published in The Independent on Friday 5 August 2011, was reproduced by permission of Steve Connor/The Independent; extract from 'Square Roots' by Ross Martin (pages 82–83), published in the Herald on Sunday 10 February 2013, was reproduced by permission of Ross Martin; extracts from *Bold Girls* by Rona Munro on pages 13–14, 51–52 and 86–87 were reproduced by permission of Nick Hern Books extracts from *Tally's Blood* by Anne-Marie Di Mambro on pages 15–16, 53–54 and 89–91 were reproduced by permission of Hodder Education; extracts from *Sailmaker* by Alan Spence on pages 18–19, 55–56 and 91–92 were reproduced by permission of Hodder Education; Extract from *The Crater* (pages 20–21), *The Telegram* (pages 58–59) and *The Painter* (pages 93–94) by Iain Crichton Smith were reproduced by permission of Birlinn Ltd; extracts from *Dear Santa* (pages 22–23), *Zimmerobics* (pages 61–62) and *A Chitterin Bite* (pages 95–96) by Anne Donovan were reproduced by permission of Canongate Books; extracts from *The Testament of Gideon Mack* by James Robertson on pages 24–25, 63–64 and 98–99 were reproduced by permission of Penguin Books Ltd; extracts from The Cone-Gatherers by Robin Jenkins on pages 29–28, 67–68 and 103–104 were reproduced by permission of Peters Fraser Dunlop; poems *Anne Hathaway* (page 32), *War Photographer* (page 69) and *Originally* (page 106) by Carol Ann Duffy were reproduced by permission of Picador; poems *Bed* (page 34), *Lucozade* (pages 71–72) and *Divorce* (page 108) by Jackie Kay were reproduced by permission of Picador; poems *Sounds of the Day* (page 36), *Assisi* (page 73) and *Aunt Julia* (pages 110–111) by Norman MacCaig were reproduced by permission of Birlinn Ltd; poems *Hyena* (page 38), *Trio* (page 75) and *Winter* (page 112) by Edwin Morgan were reproduced by permission of Carcanet Press Ltd.

Whilst every effort has been made to trace the copyright holders, in cases where this has been unsuccessful, or if any have inadvertently been overlooked, the Publishers would gladly receive any information enabling them to rectify any error or omission at the first opportunity.

Introduction

National 5 English Practice Papers

This book contains three brand new and complete question papers for National 5 English, which mirror the actual SQA exam as closely as possible in question style, level, layout and appearance. It is a perfect way to familiarise yourself with the exam papers you will sit.

The answer section at the back of the book contains fully worked answers to each question, showing you where marks are gained in an answer and how the right answer is arrived at. It is also packed with explanatory **Hints**, which explain the answers in more detail and provide essential practical tips on tackling certain question types.

The Practice Papers can be used in two ways:

1. You can complete an entire practice paper as preparation for the final exam. If you would like to use the book in this way, you can either complete the practice paper under exam-style conditions by setting yourself a time for each paper and answering it as well as possible without using any notes. Alternatively, you can answer the practice paper questions as a revision exercise, using your notes to produce model answers.

2. You can use the **topic index** on page 5 to find out which types of questions are asked within each Reading for Understanding, Analysis and Evaluation practice paper. You can also use this index to focus on a specific type of question that you want to revise.

The National 5 exam is your chance to show the skills and knowledge you have acquired in reading and writing. The key to successful preparation for exams is practice. This book will provide you with the practice you need to approach the final assessment with confidence.

The external assessment of National 5 English is divided into **Part 1: Reading for Understanding, Analysis and Evaluation** and **Part 2: Critical Reading**. Critical Reading is further divided into **Section 1: Scottish texts** and **Section 2: Critical essay**.

Part 1: Reading for Understanding, Analysis and Evaluation

This is the paper which in Standard Grade, Intermediate and Higher English was known as Close Reading. You will be required to read a non-fiction passage and answer questions. The passage may be a newspaper or magazine article, an extract from a piece of travel writing or biography.

The questions will cover these three areas:

- Showing your **understanding** of the passage by putting things in your own words, summarising and selecting key ideas.

- **Analysing** the way the writer conveys these ideas through techniques such as word choice, imagery, sentence structure and tone.

- **Evaluating** how effectively the writer conveys these ideas, giving your opinion about the writer's use of language.

Part 2: Critical Reading

Section 1: Scottish texts

In this part of the exam you will be given an extract from the text or texts you have studied in class. This part of the paper asks you to combine two related skills:

1. Why is this extract important? What ideas does it present? How is language used?

2. How does the extract fit into the whole text or set of texts? For example, what themes or ideas in the extract relate to other stories or poems by the same writer?

Section 2: Critical essay

Here you will have approximately 45 minutes to answer a question on a text you have studied in class. There will be a choice of questions covering different genres: drama, prose, poetry and film and TV drama or language study. You will be asked to focus on one aspect of your chosen text. To be able to write a well-structured, detailed answer to the question you will need to know the text fully.

This book will help you to go into the exam prepared to demonstrate your knowledge and skills. Use it for timed practice, for focused study and to guide your revision.

Topic Index for Reading for Understanding, Analysis and Evaluation practice papers

Topic	Paper A	Paper B	Paper C	Knowledge for Prelim			Knowledge for SQA Exam		
				Having difficulty	Still needs work	Ok	Having difficulty	Still needs work	Ok
In your own words	1, 3, 7, 8	1(a), 2, 3, 4, 5, 6	1(a), 2, 3, 4, 7						
Language	2								
Word choice	4	1(b)	1(b), 5						
Rhetorical questions	5								
Writer's attitude	6		6						
Effective conclusion	9	7							
Imagery	8	8	8						
Key points	10	9	9						

Practice Exam A

Practice Papers for SQA Exams

ENGLISH

NATIONAL 5

Exam A

Reading for Understanding, Analysis and Evaluation

Date — Not applicable

Duration — 1 hour

Total marks: 30

Read the extract and then answer the questions in your own words as much as possible. Try to answer all of the questions.

Scotland's leading educational publishers

What sport tells us about life

This extract is taken from a book by writer and former cricketer Ed Smith, in which he investigates the sociology and psychology of sport.

What kind of fan are you?

Have you paid a small fortune to be one of 76,000 watching Manchester United at Old Trafford? Or are you a loyal supporter of a tiny team, a bigger cog in an infinitely smaller wheel? Perhaps you are nervously hiding behind a tree, hoping not to convey your anxiety to your already
5   panicky son as he gets marooned on 99 in a school cricket match.

What are you doing here? Take your eyes off the pitch for a moment and look around. Glance at the rows of people, whether they are sitting on the recreation park bench or in an international stadium – some may have planned this moment as the centrepiece of their month, others may merely be distracting themselves to avoid weekend boredom. How can one activity – sport –
10   unite such disparate strands of humanity? What on earth have they come to find?

We imagine it is straightforward: everyone sees the same match, even through different eyes. But, in truth, we all have a unique 'take' on sport that means we experience it in an individual way. Perspective is everything.

There is much talk in the sports world about 'experts' and 'mere fans', as though there is an
15   inner caste of privileged insiders who know what is going on. It isn't true. Sports fans of limited knowledge but acute perceptiveness sometimes have far deeper insights about the game than people who are unhealthily obsessed.

The difference between an 'expert' and a 'mere fan' revolves around knowledge – who knows the most. But many of the characteristics which really separate sports fans have nothing to do with
20   degrees of learning. Instead, they derive from differences in temperament. It is temperament that determines how you watch sport, what you see as you do so, which parts of your personality the stuff reaches, how deep it goes and why you come back for more.

One of sport's wonders is the breadth of its support. I use breadth carefully, not meaning simply that lots of people like it – the popularity of sport is well known. Instead I mean the coming
25   together of diametrically differing types of people, all glued to the same pitch or television screen. Some fans love the expectation more than the match itself. Others revel in the spectacle and the sense of theatre. To many supporters, sport is about belonging – to a team, a club or a community of fans. A different type is more detached, imagining himself as the manager or captain, looking down on the melee and searching for the right strategy. More common, I
30   expect, is the fan who watches the match like a reader gripped by the narrative of a novel, simply wondering what will happen next.

But there is another huge category of fan: people who just love a bloody good argument. Sport gets them there. It makes them think, engage and argue. Sport stimulates and challenges. It *provokes* them. We know that playing sport is pugilistic; perhaps following sport can be as well.

35   Sports fans argue about anything and everything. Is too much money bad for sport? Given they've got all these damned statistics, why do they keep picking the wrong team? If the standard of sport is improving, why do today's players seem less good than yesterday's giants? What part does luck play in top-class sport?

Unravel the ideas behind the arguments in those few sentences and you will find questions
40 about evolution, destiny, psychology, the free market, history and many other disciplines.

That might sound daunting, but it should be liberating. Sport can be enjoyed at lots of different
levels – just like music, literature or art. You don't have to take an intellectual or analytical
approach to love it. If you turn the pages of the novel simply to find out what happens next you
are still getting your money's worth. But potentially there is also a deeper level of enjoyment.

45 So it is with sport. I am not arguing that you should care more about sport in the conventional
sense of sitting *even* longer with your head in your hands while your team crashes to defeat. In
many ways we already take it more than earnestly enough. But given that people already take
sport so very seriously, and at such an intense level of enquiry, then we might as well draw out
some of sport's intellectual lessons and practical uses while we're arguing about it. Sport, I think,
50 is a huge and mostly unused analytical resource.

Sport has a rich conceptual framework, if only we would open our eyes to it. If you want to prove
how much luck intervenes in our history, sport is the perfect place to start the enquiry. If you
want to know how to change an institution, sport has great examples. Sport pits nature against
nurture and lets us all watch and take sides. If you wonder about the limits of objectivity, sport
55 raises the question of the relationship between facts and opinion. Sport invites nostalgia about a
mythic golden age, then mocks it by holding up a stopwatch that shows ever-improving world-
record times.

We see what we want to see when we watch sport. The angry fan finds tribal belonging; the
pessimist sees steady decline and fall; the optimist hails progress in each innovation; the
60 sympathetic soul feels every blow and disappointment; the rationalist wonders how the haze of
illogical thinking endures.

From the players and the fans to the institutions and the record books, sport is full of prejudices,
perspectives and historical changes – the unavoidable stuff of life. Sport is a condensed version of
life – only it matters less and comes up with better statistics.

Adapted from What Sport Tells Us About Life, by Ed Smith.

Questions

1. **In your own words**, what kinds of fans does the writer describe in the second paragraph?   2

2. Look at lines 6–17. How does the writer's language make clear the different ways that people feel about following sport?   4

3. **In your own words**, say what the 'differing types of people' are that the writer describes in lines 23–34.   4

4. Look at lines 32–34. Explain how the writer's word choice makes clear the response of the fans who 'like a bloody good argument.'   2

5. Choose **one** of the rhetorical questions from lines 35–38 and discuss its effect.   2

6. Look at lines 41–44. Identify the writer's attitude to sport in this paragraph and give evidence to support your answer.   2

7. Look at lines 51–57. **In your own words**, explain what lessons the writer believes we can take from sport.   3

8. Look at lines 58–61. **In your own words**, explain how different types of people find different things in sport.   4

9. Look at lines 62–64. How does the final paragraph provide an effective conclusion to the passage? Give evidence to support your answer.   3

10. Referring to the whole article, in your own words list the key points the writer makes about sport.   4

[END OF QUESTION PAPER]

Practice
Papers for
SQA Exams

ENGLISH
NATIONAL 5
Exam A
Critical Reading

Date — Not applicable

Duration — 1 hour and 30 minutes

Total marks: 40

Section A: Scottish Text – 20 marks

Choose an extract from a Scottish text you have studied and then answer the questions. Try to complete all of the questions.

Choose only **one** text from either Part A Drama, Part B Prose or Part C Poetry.

Section B: Critical Essay – 20 marks

Write **one** critical essay on a text you have studied from one of the genres of Drama, Prose, Poetry, Film and TV Drama or Language Study.

You are permitted to write an essay on a text from the list of Scottish texts, providing that you have not written about the same text in Section A and that the genre you select is not the same as the one you answered on in Section A.

Each section of the exam should take approximately 45 minutes to complete.

Section A — Scottish Text — 20 marks

Answer the questions from **one** of the three sections only (Drama, Prose or Poetry).

Read the text carefully and then answer **all** of the questions on the text, writing the answers in your own words as much as possible.

SCOTTISH TEXT (DRAMA)

If you choose to write on this text in Section A you may not write a critical essay on drama in Section B.

Read the extract below and then attempt the following questions.

Text 1

Bold Girls **by Rona Munro**

Scene one

Marie's house. Belfast. Late afternoon. Present day.

It is irons and ironing boards and piles of clothes waiting to be smoothed, socks and pegs and damp sheets waiting for a break in the Belfast drizzle for the line; it's toys in pieces and toys that are just cardboard boxes and toys that are new and gleaming and flashing with lights and have swallowed up
5 *this year's savings. It's pots and pans and steam and the kettle always hot for tea; it's furniture that's bald with age and a hearth in front of the coal fire that's gleaming clean.*

At the moment it's empty, an unnatural, expectant emptiness that suggests this room is never deserted; it's too stuffed with human bits and pieces, all the clutter of housework and life.

There is a small picture of the Virgin on one wall, a large grainy blow-up photo of a smiling young man
10 *on the other. He has a seventies haircut and moustache.*

Deirdre is not in this room, she's crouching on all fours on her own, talking out of darkness in which only her face is visible. She is wary, young.

DEIRDRE: *(moving from all fours)* The sun is going down behind the hills, the sky is grey. There's hills at the back, green. I can't hardly see them because the stones here and there are grey, the street is grey. Somewhere a bird is singing and falling in the sky.
15 I hear the ice cream van and the traffic and the helicopter overhead.

Blackout; after a few minutes lights come up on Marie's house.

Marie bursts into the room with her arms laden with four packets of crisps, two packs of Silk Cut and a packet of chocolate biscuits. She is cheerful, efficient, young. She drops one of the crisps, tuts in
20 *exasperation, and looks at it.*

MARIE: *(shouting back out the door)* Mickey! Mickey were you wanting smoky bacon? Well this is salt and vinegar…Well, why did you not say? Away you and swap this… Catch now. No you cannot…No…because you'll not eat your tea if you do! *(At the doorway)* Mickey, pick up those crisps and don't be so bold.

25   *Marie comes back into the room and starts two jobs simultaneously. First she puts the crisps etc. away, then she fills a pan with water and throws it on the stove. She starts sorting her dry washing into what needs ironing and what doesn't; she sorts a few items then starts peeling potatoes; all her movements have a frenetic efficiency.*

Questions

1. **In your own words**, summarise the setting as described in the stage directions in lines 1–10.   3

2. Look at the lines relating to Deirdre, 11–16. How does the word choice help to create mystery and menace?   2

3. What impression of Marie is revealed in this extract through word choice in stage directions and dialogue?   4

4. Male characters do not appear on stage, either in this extract or in the rest of the play. However, male characters are mentioned here: the picture in the stage directions (Michael) and Mickey. Comment on the playwright's portrayal of the male characters in this extract.   3

5. In this extract Deirdre is still not a part of Marie's life. With close reference to the rest of the play, explain her impact on the other characters and the ideas this helps to convey.   8

If you choose to write on this text in Section A you may not write a critical essay on drama in Section B.

Read the extract below and then attempt the following questions.

Text 2

***Tally's Blood* by Anne-Marie di Mambro**

MASSIMO:	My faither's got a house in Italy. I've no been back since we got Lucia. Her dad's supposed to look after it for us. You know what that means! It's just got the two rooms, bare walls, bare floors, and the hens march in and out all day long. There's no hot water, no cludgie, no lights, no gas. You've to walk two miles for water and cook on a big black pot on the fire. If you want a keigh you've got to go outside. There's a hole in the ground with a plank across it and the flies buzz around your arse. *(A beat)* God, I wish I was there now.
ROSINELLA:	*(Screams)* Massimo!
	Massimo runs to her.
MASSIMO:	*(Shouts)* Lucia.
	Lucia runs up to them.
LUCIA:	What's wrong?
ROSINELLA:	*(To Massimo)* Shut the shop up. Quick.
	Massimo rushes out to front shop. Rosinella grabs Lucia.
ROSINELLA:	Lucia, my darling, I want you to do everything your Uncle Massimo says. You have to be brave. For me.
LUCIA:	What's happening?
ROSINELLA:	You're too wee to really understand, but Italy is in the war against this country and the people are taking it out on the Italians.
	Massimo in: Lucia runs to him.
LUCIA:	Uncle Massimo, I'm frightened.
MASSIMO:	It's alright darling, your Uncle Massimo's here.
ROSINELLA:	Get the black-outs up quick.
MASSIMO:	They're up.
ROSINELLA:	We better shift some stuff. You come give me a hand, Lucia. You get the cigarettes, Massimo, take them upstairs.
	Lucia and Rosinella go into front shop.
MASSIMO:	Rosie, get back in here.
	Rosinella and Lucia in, each carrying boxes of sweeties.
MASSIMO:	What you doing?

The line numbers in the left margin read: 5, 10, 15, 20, 25, 30.

	ROSINELLA:	Get these upstairs. Quick. Hide as much as we can. They'll waste everything.
	MASSIMO:	No, Rosie, leave it. Let them take what they like, waste what they like. So long as they leave you two alone.
	ROSINELLA:	*(Shocked)* Massimo! You don't think…surely? They'll no touch us!
35		*Noise of brick bashing against boards: the 'mob' outside, banging on the doors and windows: shouting.*
	MOB:	Get the Tallies!
		Fascist bastards!
40		*Lucia starts to weep, frightened. Rosinella holds her, crouches with her. The level of noise increases:*
		Rosinella trying to shoosh Lucia: Massimo looking round him in despair: Rosinella putting a restraining hand on his arm.
	MOB:	Get the bastard.
		Waste the place.
45		Fascist pigs.
		Greasy Tallies.
	MASSIMO:	*(Whispers)* They cannie do this to me.
	ROSINELLA:	*(Whispers)* Massimo…please…don't do anything. Please, please.
		Jeers continue.
50	MOB:	Come out and fight you bastarding Tally!
	ROSINELLA:	Oh Sant' Antonio. San Guiseppe.
		Massimo makes to go to the door.
	MASSIMO:	I can't just stand here and do nothing.
	ROSINELLA:	Massimo…no! Don't leave us.
55		*She holds on to his arm as they break into front shop: we see their silhouettes carrying sticks and stones. We see and hear the smashing up and the jeers.*

Questions

6. **In your own words**, summarise what happens in this extract from the play. Make at least **three** points.

    3

7. Massimo humorously shows that he misses Italy at the beginning of the extract. Show how the language of this section, lines 1–7, creates this humour.

    4

8. What is the mood or atmosphere of this extract and how does the writer use language effectively to create this mood or atmosphere?

    3

9. How does the language of the extract make clear Lucia's relationship with either: Rosinella **or** Massimo?

    2

10. The experience of immigrants is an important theme in this extract. With close reference to the rest of the play, show how this theme is explored.

    8

If you choose to write on this text in Section A you may not write a critical essay on drama in Section B.

Read the extract below and then attempt the following questions.

Text 3

***Sailmaker* by Alan Spence**

	DAVIE:	It's hard son. It's no easy on your own.
	ALEC:	So ye go an get bevvied. Forget it all.
	DAVIE:	Ye'd think ah came in steamin every night!
5		Christ ah need a wee break once in a while. Like the night. Nae harm in it. Good company. Wee sing song. Right gents, a wee bit order there. One singer, one song. That lassie Peggy's a rare singer. Sang Honky Tonk Angels.
		She's the one ah told ye about.
	ALEC:	(*Sarcastic*) The really nice person.
	DAVIE:	She wis.
10	ALEC:	Who was that lady I saw you with last night?
		That was no lady, that was a really nice person.
	DAVIE:	Nae harm in it.
	ALEC:	It's always the same. Every time ye meet a wumman she's a really really really nice person.
15		Why don't ye just admit that ye fancy her?
		(*DAVIE slaps him, exits*)
		Ach aye, yirra good boy son. Wallop!
		Bad. Bad. Bad.
		(*Pause*)
20		Wallop.
		(*Darkness. Spotlight on Alec*)
		I keep goin back.
		What is it I'm tryin to remember?
		What is it I'm tryin to say?
25		There's somethin I've lost. Something I've forgotten.
		Sometimes in the middle of the night…
		What is it I'm lookin for?
		God knows.

(Lights up. He crosses over, picks up yacht. DAVIE is sitting in chair, staring into empty hearth)

30

Remember this?

DAVIE: Eh? *(Looks)* Oh aye.

It's freezing.

ALEC: Nae coal left?

35   DAVIE: Ah'll get some themorra, when the dole money comes.

ALEC: Ye wouldnae believe some of the stuff that's in the Glory Hole.

DAVIE: Is that where ye wur? Terrible draught comin in that door.

ALEC: Hey, d'ye remember that poem ye used to tell me?

DAVIE: Poem?

40   ALEC: About the yacht. *(Recites)*

Ah had a yacht

Y'ought tae see it

I actually thought you wrote it, ye know – made it up yourself.

DAVIE: Och naw. Ah learned it fae *ma* father. Ah wis just passin it on.

Questions

11. **In your own words**, summarise the conflict between Davie and Alec in the extract.   **4**

12. With close reference to the text, explain how the playwright conveys the character and emotions of the two characters in this extract:

     (a) Davie   **2**

     (b) Alec   **2**

13. Comment on two examples of the playwright's use of stage directions and lighting in this extract to convey mood and character.   **4**

14. This extract marks an important stage in the development of the relationship between Davie and Alec. With close reference to the text, explain how relationships between fathers and sons are explored in the play.   **8**

SCOTTISH TEXT (PROSE)

If you choose to write on this text in Section A you may not write a critical essay on prose in Section B.

Read the extract below and then attempt the following questions.

Text 1

The Crater by Iain Crichton Smith

In this extract, set during World War One, Lieutenant Robert McKinnon and his men attempt to rescue another soldier from a flooded crater.

He stopped. 'All right,' he said. 'We're going for him. Come on.'

And he stood up. There was no reason for crawling any more. The night was clear. And they would have to hurry. And the other two stood up as well when they saw him doing so. He couldn't leave a man to die in the pit of green slime. 'We'll run,' he said. And they ran to the first one and
5 listened. They cried fiercely, 'Are you there?' But there was no answer. Then they seemed to hear it from the next one and they were at that one soon too, peering down into the green slime, illuminated by moonlight. But there was no answer. There was one left and they made for that one. They screamed again, in the sound of the shells, and they seemed to hear an answer. There was one left and they made for that one. They screamed again, in the sound of the shells, and
10 they seemed to hear an answer. They heard what seemed to be a bubbling. 'Are you there?' said Robert, bending down and listening. 'Can you get over here?' They could hear splashing and deep below them breathing, frantic breathing as if someone was frightened to death. 'It's all right,' he said, 'if you come over here, I'll send my rifle down. You two hang on to me,' he said to the others. He was terrified. That depth, that green depth. Was it Morrison down there, after all?
15 He hadn't spoken. The splashings came closer. The voice was like an animal's repeating endlessly a mixture of curses and prayers. Robert hung over the edge of a crater, 'For Christ's sake don't let me go,' he said to the other two. It wasn't right that a man should die in green slime. He hung over the rim holding his rifle down. He felt it being caught, as if there was a great fish at the end of a line. He felt it moving. And the others hung at his heels, like a chain. The moon shone
20 suddenly out between two clouds and in that moment he saw it, a body covered with greenish slime, an obscene mermaid, hanging on to his rifle while the two eyes, white in the green face, shone upward and the mouth, gritted, tried not to let the blood through. It was a monster of the deep, it was a sight so terrible that he nearly fell. He was about to say, 'It's no good, he's dying,' but something prevented him from saying it, if he said it then he would never forget it. He knew that.
25 The hands clung to the rifle below in the slime. The others pulled behind him. 'For Christ's sake hang on to the rifle,' he said to the monster below. 'Don't let go.' And it seemed to be emerging from the deep, setting its feet against the side of the crater, all green, all mottled, like a disease. It climbed up as if up a mountainside in the stench. It hung there against the wall. 'Hold on,' he said. 'Hold on.' His whole body was concentrated. This man must not fall down again into that
30 lake. The death would be too terrible. The face was coming over the side of the crater, the teeth gritted, blood at the mouth. It hung there for a long moment and then the three of them had got him over the side. He felt like cheering, standing up in the light of No Man's Land and cheering.

Sergeant Smith was kneeling down beside the body, his ear to the heart. It was like a body which might have come from space, green and illuminated and shiny. And over it poured the
35 merciless moonlight.

'Come on,' he said to the other two. And at that moment Sergeant Smith said, 'He's dead.'

Questions

15. Summarise what happens in this extract from the short story. Make at least **three** key points.

3

16. Look at lines 2–35. What mood or atmosphere is created by the writer and how does the writer use language effectively to create this mood or atmosphere?

3

17. Look at lines 26–35. Show how any **two** examples of the writer's use of language to describe the soldier Robert is rescuing contribute to the reader's response.

4

18. Look at the final paragraph. What effect does this have and how does the writer's use of language contribute to this effect?

2

19. By referring to this extract and the story *The Crater* as a whole, explain how the ideas/language are similar **or** different to at least **one** other story by Iain Crichton Smith that you have read.

8

If you choose to write on this text in Section A you may not write a critical essay on prose in Section B.

Read the extract below and then attempt the following questions.

Text 2

***Dear Santa* by Anne Donovan**

In this extract the narrator, Alison, is a young girl who is writing her letter to Santa Claus.

Christmas Eve ah'm sittin on the bed in ma pyjamas wi a pad of blue lined paper and a Biro. The room is daurk but the wee bedside lamp makes a white circle that lights up the page ah'm starin at. It's hard tae find the words.

Dear Santa,

5   *Please could you*

I would like

If it's no too much bother

But what is it ah'm trying tae say? Could you make ma mammy love me? That's no Santa's job, he's there tae gie oot sweeties and toys tae weans wanst a year, so there's nae point in askin him. If
10   there is a Santa. Ah look oot the windae; the sky's dirty grey and ah don't think we'll huv a white Christmas somehow.

The door opens and ma mammy comes in. The hall light's on and her hair sticks oot all roon her heid, fuzzy and soft. A cannae see her face.

Are you no asleep yet? It's nine o'clock.

15   *Ah'm writin ma letter tae Santa.*

Santa doesnae come if yer no sleepin. Look, there's Katie, soond.

She bends ower Katie's bed, where she's lyin wi wan airm stickin oot fae under the covers. Ma mammy lifts the bedclothes over her, then turns tae me.

Hurry up and finish that letter, Alison. Ah'll pit in fronty the fire and Santa'll get it when he comes.

20   Ma mammy sits on the bed beside me while ah take a clean bit of paper and write dead slow so it's ma best writin.

Dear Santa,

Please could I have a Barbie doll and a toy dog, I am a good girl.

Love

25   *Alison*

Ah fold the paper twice, print SANTA on the front, then gie it tae ma mammy. She pits it in her pocket and lifts the covers fur me tae get inside. Ah coorie, watchin her hair glowin like a halo against the blackness of the room. Ah love stroking her hair, it's that soft and fuzzy but she cannae be bothered wi that and jerks her heid away, sayin *don't, you'll mess it up,* just lik she
30   does when ma daddy tries tae touch it. But it's that quiet and still and she's in a good mood so ah lift ma haun and touch her hair, just a wee bit.

Mammy, how come you've got fair hair and Katie's got fair hair and mine's is broon?

You take efter yer daddy and Katie takes efter me.

Ah wisht ah had fair hair.

35   *How? There's nothing wrang wi broon hair.*

Ah wisht ah had hair like yours.

Ma mammy smiles and the lines roon her eyes get deeper but she looks at me mair soft like.

Go tae sleep, hen, or Santa'll no come.

She bends ower and kisses me, a dry kiss, barely grazin ma cheek, and before ah have time tae
40   kiss her back she's switched off the bedside light, stood up and moved tae the door.

Night, Alison.

Night, Mammy.

She goes oot, nearly closing the door, but leavin a wee crack of light fallin across the bedclothes.

Questions

20. Summarise what happens in this extract from the short story. Make at least **three** key points.

    3

21. Look at lines 1–11. What is the mood of the narrator and how does the writer use language to convey this mood?

    3

22. Look at lines 12–36. Show how any **two** examples of the writer's use of language convey the relationship between Alison and her mother.

    4

23. Look at lines 37–44. In your opinion how does Alison feel at the end of the story? Quote and comment to support your answer.

    2

24. By referring to this extract and the story *Dear Santa* as a whole, explain how the ideas/language are similar OR different to at least **one** other story by Anne Donovan that you have read.

    8

If you choose to write on this text in Section A you may not write a critical essay on prose in Section B.

Read the extract below and then attempt the following questions.

Text 3

***The Testament of Gideon Mack* by James Robertson**

In this extract, Gideon Mack's father, Reverend James Mack, discovers Gideon watching television on a Sunday, which he has previously forbidden.

Thus we stood in front of the television together, father and son, for the remaining ten minutes of the programme. It felt like an hour. If I squirmed to ease the pain, his grip tightened. I hated him then, hated what he was doing to me and hated my own helplessness. *ZAP! BLAM! POW!* I hated the screen with its cartoon punches and I hated the way the parlour echoed with screeching tyres and
5   wisecracks delivered in American accents. I saw it as if through his eyes – cheap, tawdry, meaningless rubbish – and I longed for it to end.

He pushed me from him as the credits rolled and the inane theme music played. 'Turn it off,' he said. I did as I was told, rubbing my neck and wiping away the tears that he had squeezed out of me.

10   'What…is…that?' he said, dropping the words methodically into the silence.

'*Batman*,' I said.

'Bat…man,' he said.

'Yes,' I said. And then again, 'I'm sorry.' But I don't think he heard that.

'It is not bat…man,' he said, and I could not stop myself, I was trying to explain, I said, 'It is.'

15   'Do not interrupt me,' he said. His voice grew louder and harder. 'Do not contradict me. It is not bat…man, whatever that means. I'll tell you what it is. It is drivel. It is the most unutterable garbage I have ever witnessed. Garbage from the land of garbage. I can hardly credit that you have opened your mind to such trash, that you have defiled the brain God gave you with it. But then…' – he was gathering himself, I could feel the storm coming – 'but then, to have played this
20   game of deceit, to have lied to me…'

'I haven't lied,' I said, but the storm broke and I was muttering into a mighty wind.

'You have lied, Gideon,' he roared, 'and you know it full well. You have betrayed me and you have betrayed God with your creeping and your skulking, your wallowing in that filth. You have taken your sin into a corner to play with, guilt all over your face. You have disgraced this house and you
25   have sullied this day, that is God's day and his alone. How can you have done this under my roof, Gideon? I can hardly bear to look at you. The very sight of you makes me sick.'

Even at this distance I remember all those words. He was so angry, so revolted, that he did indeed turn his head from me, keeping his eye fixed on the television set. I wonder now what he was seeing: perhaps his own reflection in the dead screen, a parody of a ranting minister, or a man

30   in a fable seeing his own son corrupted by the magical box he himself had brought home. To be told by your father that the sight of you offends him is a terrible thing. The contempt in his voice sounded as though it would last for ever. Which it has. Here I am, four decades on, and I can still hear it.

Tears streamed from my eyes, but I wasn't crying, I was too shocked for that. I stood as still as I
35   could, waiting to be struck. He hardly ever hit me: his hands were so big and hard that I took great care to avoid giving him reason to do so. But if he did it was over in seconds, a few heavy, stinging blows on my backside with the flat of his hand or a stick. I could have taken a beating with a stick, but I feared what he might do if he attacked me again with his hands. I stood there on the edge of something unknown, waiting for him to act.

40   The door opened. My mother appeared, wrapped in her fawn dressing-gown. 'James,' she said. And then, 'Gideon.'

He turned on her furiously. 'What do you want?'

'Your voice woke me,' she said. 'What is going on?'

'Nothing,' he said, 'except that this boy, your son, has defiled this house, the Lord's day and
45   himself. I am dealing with it. Go away!'

'I don't think…' she began.

'Get out!'

I expected her to scurry away, but she didn't. She had seen something that I did not, something peculiar perhaps in the blotches on his face or the tremor of his body. Then she did what I had
50   never seen her do before: she reached out her hand to him.

'James,' she said. 'Please calm yourself. You will do yourself an injury.'

'I will do *you*…an injury,' he said and his right arm came up as if to hit her. At that point I too realised that something was far wrong, for though he thought my mother stupid he had never raised a hand to her. His threat sounded empty, like a line in a play delivered by an actor who
55   doesn't understand it. His voice went up at the end, more like a question, and his hand stayed high, quivering where he had raised it.

'Are you all right, James?' my mother said.

'Why?' he said. 'Don't I look all right?' And the next thing he crumpled in a heap on the floor, all six feet of him folding like a collapsible wooden ruler.

60   I stood there like a statue, or an imbecile, convinced that it was I who had delivered the blow that had felled him.

'Gideon,' my mother said, suddenly efficient as she knelt down beside him. 'Phone for an ambulance. Dial 999. Quickly now.'

My father convulsed and a little pile of yellow vomit appeared on the carpet by his mouth. That
65   was the thing that unshocked me and set me free again. I ran to the telephone.

Questions

25. Summarise what happens in this extract from the novel Make at least **three** key points.

3

26. Look at paragraph 1 (lines 1–6). What is the mood of the narrator in this paragraph, and how does the writer use language effectively to convey this mood?

3

27. Look at lines 15–26. Show how **two** examples of the writer's use of language convey James Mack's feelings towards his son.

4

28. Look at lines 48–65. How does the writer's use of language create a sense of climax at the end of this extract?

2

29. By referring to this extract, and to at least **two** other incidents from elsewhere in the novel, explain how the relationship between Gideon and his father develops and how this influences Gideon.

8

If you choose to write on this text in Section A you may not write a critical essay on prose in Section B.

Read the extract below and then attempt the following questions.

Text 4

Kidnapped **by Robert Louis Stevenson**

In this extract, which is from Chapter 10, 'The siege of the round-house', Alan Breck and the narrator, David Balfour, are on board the Covenant *and are fighting off the seamen who wish to kill Breck.*

Then there came a single call on the sea-pipe, and that was the signal. A knot of them made one rush of it, cutlass in hand, against the door; and at the same moment, the glass of the skylight was dashed in a thousand pieces, and a man leaped through and landed on the floor. Before he got his feet, I had clapped a pistol to his back, and might have shot him, too; only at the touch of
5   him (and him alive) my whole flesh misgave me, and I could no more pull the trigger than I could have flown.

He had dropped his cutlass as he jumped, and when he felt the pistol, whipped straight round and laid hold of me, roaring out an oath; and at that either my courage came again, or I grew so much afraid as came to the same thing; for I gave a shriek and shot him in the midst of the body.
10   He gave the most horrible, ugly groan and fell to the floor. The foot of a second fellow, whose legs were dangling through the skylight, struck me at the same time upon the head; and at that I snatched another pistol and shot this one through the thigh, so that he slipped through and tumbled in a lump on his companion's body. There was no talk of missing, any more than there was time to aim; I clapped the muzzle to the very place and fired.

15   I might have stood and stared at them for long, but I heard Alan shout as if for help, and that brought me to my senses.

He had kept the door so long; but one of the seamen, while he was engaged with others, had run in under his guard and caught him about the body. Alan was dirking him with his left hand, but the fellow clung like a leech. Another had broken in and had his cutlass raised. The door was
20   thronged with their faces. I thought we were lost, and catching up my cutlass, fell on them in flank.

But I had not time to be of help. The wrestler dropped at last; and Alan, leaping back to get his distance, ran upon the others like a bull, roaring as he went. They broke before him like water, turning, and running, and falling one against another in their haste. The sword in his hands
25   flashed like quicksilver into the huddle of our fleeing enemies; and at every flash there came the scream of a man hurt. I was still thinking we were lost, when lo! they were all gone, and Alan was driving them along the deck as a sheep-dog chases sheep.

Yet he was no sooner out than he was back again, being as cautious as he was brave; and meanwhile the seamen continued running and crying out as if he was still behind them; and we
30   heard them tumble one upon another into the forecastle, and clap-to the hatch upon the top.

The round-house was like a shambles; three were dead inside, another lay in his death agony across the threshold; and there were Alan and I victorious and unhurt.

He came up to me with open arms. 'Come to my arms!' he cried, and embraced and kissed me hard upon both cheek. 'David,' said he, 'I love you like a brother. And O, man,' he cried in a kind
35 of ecstasy, 'am I no a bonny fighter?'

Thereupon he turned to the four enemies, passed his sword clean through each of them, and tumbled them out of doors one after the other. As he did so, he kept humming and singing and whistling to himself, like a man trying to recall an air; only what HE was trying was to make one. All the while, the flush was in his face, and… And presently he sat down upon the table,
40 sword in hand; the air that he was making all the time began to run a little clearer, and then clearer still; and then out he burst with a great voice into a Gaelic song.

Questions

30. Summarise what happens in this extract from the novel. Make at least **four** key points.

4

31. Look at lines 3–16. Show how the writer uses language effectively to portray the mood of the narrator in these lines.

2

32. Look at lines 17–32. How does the writer convey the violence and action of this extract?

4

33. Look again at lines 36–41. How does the writer portray the character of Alan Breck in these lines?

2

34. By referring to this extract, and to at least **two** other incidents from elsewhere in the novel, explain how the relationship between David Balfour and Alan Breck changes and develops as the story progresses.

8

Read the extract below and then attempt the following questions.

Text 5

***The Cone-Gatherers* by Robin Jenkins**

It was Calum who first saw the deer.

The drive was nearly over. Only a hundred or so yards away were the waiting guns. Frightened by the noises approaching them from the rear, and apprehensive of the human silence ahead, the five roe deer were halted, their heads high in nervous alertness. When Calum saw them,
5 his cry was of delight and friendship, and then of terrified warning as the dogs too, and Duror, caught sight of them and rushed in pursuit. Silently, with marvellous grace and agility over such rough ground, the deer flew for the doom ahead. Their white behinds were like moving glints of sunlight; without them their tawny hides might not have been seen in the autumnal wood.

Calum no longer was one of the beaters; he too was a deer hunted by remorseless men. Moaning
10 and gasping, he fled after them, with no hope of saving them from slaughter but with the impulse to share it with them. He could not, however, be so swift or sure of foot. He fell and rose again; he avoided one tree only to collide with another close to it; and all the time he felt, as the deer must have, the indifference of all nature; of the trees, of tall withered stalks of willowherb, of the patches of blue sky, of bushes, of piles of cut scrubwood, of birds lurking in branches, and of
15 the sunlight: presences which might have been expected to help or at least sympathise.

The dogs barked fiercely. Duror fired his gun in warning to those waiting in the ride. Neil, seeing his brother rush into the danger, roared to him to come back. All the beaters, except Charlie far in the rear, joined in the commotion; the wood resounded with their exultant shouts. Realising this must be the finish or kill, Graham, recuperating on the road, hopped back over the fence into the
20 wood and bellowed loudest of all.

As Duror bawled to his dogs to stop lest they interfere with the shooting, and as the deer hesitated before making the dash across the ride, Calum was quite close to them as, silent, desperate and heroic, they sprang forward to die or escape. When the guns banged he did not, as Neil had vehemently warned him to do, fall flat on the ground and put his fingers in his ears.
25 Instead, with wails of lament, he dashed on at demented speed and shot out onto the broad green ride to hear a deer screaming and see it, wounded in the breast and forelegs, scrabbling about on its hindquarters. Captain Forgan was feverishly reloading his gun to fire again. Calum saw no one else, not even the lady or Mr Tulloch, who was standing by himself about twenty yards away.

30 Screaming in sympathy, heedless of the danger of being shot, Calum flung himself upon the deer, clasped it round the neck, and tried to comfort it. Terrified more than ever, it dragged him about with it in its mortal agony. Its blood came off onto his face and hands.

While Captain Forgan, young Roderick, and Lady Runcie-Campbell stood petrified by this sight, Duror followed by his dogs came leaping out of the wood. He seemed to be laughing in some
35 kind of berserk joy. There was a knife in his hand. His mistress shouted to him: what it was she did not know herself, and he never heard. Rushing upon the stricken deer and the frantic hunchback, he threw the latter off with furious force, and then, seizing the former's head with one hand cut its throat savagely with the other. Blood spouted. Lady Runcie-Campbell closed her eyes. Captain Forgan shook his head slightly in some kind of denial. Roderick screamed at Duror. Tulloch had
40 gone running over to Calum.

The deer was dead, but Duror did not rise triumphant; he crouched beside it, on his knees, as if he was mourning over it. His hands were red with blood; in one of them he still held the knife.

There were more gunshots and shouts further down the ride.

It was Tulloch who hurried to Duror to verify or disprove the suspicion that had paralysed
45 the others.

He disproved it. Duror was neither dead nor hurt.

Duror muttered something, too much of a mumble to be understood. His eyes were shut. Tulloch bent down to sniff; but he was wrong, there was no smell of whisky, only of the deer's sweat and blood. All the same, he thought, Duror had the appearance of a drunk man, unshaven, slack-
50 mouthed, mumbling, rather glaikit.

Lady Runcie-Campbell came forward, with involuntary grimaces of distaste. She avoided looking at the hunchback, seated now against the bole of a tree, sobbing like a child, his face smeared with blood.

'Has he hurt himself?' she asked of Tulloch.

55 'I don't think so, my lady. He seems to have collapsed.'

Graham came panting down the ride.

His mistress turned round and saw him.

'Oh, Graham,' she said, 'please be so good as to drag this beast away.'

Graham glanced at deer and keeper. Which beast, your ladyship? he wanted to ask. Instead, he
60 caught the deer by a hind leg and pulled it along the grass, leaving a trail of blood.

Questions

35. Summarise what happens in this extract from the novel. Make at least **three** key points.

3

36. Look at lines 1–15. The natural world is important to the novel. How does the writer portray nature in these paragraphs and how does the writer use language effectively to convey this portrayal?

3

37. Look at lines 16–32. Show how any **two** examples of the writer's use of language contribute to a growing sense of dread.

4

38. Look at Graham's thoughts in lines 56–60. From Duror's behaviour up to this point, why is this question from Graham appropriate?

2

39. By referring to this extract, and to at least **two** other incidents from elsewhere in the novel, explain how the character of Duror changes and develops as the story progresses.

8

SCOTTISH TEXT (POETRY)

If you choose to write on this text in Section A you may not write a critical essay on poetry in Section B.

Read the poem below and then attempt the following questions.

Text 1

Anne Hathaway **by Carol Ann Duffy**

'Item I gyve unto my wife my second best bed ...'
(from Shakespeare's will)

    The bed we loved in was a spinning world
    of forests, castles, torchlight, clifftops, seas
5   where we would dive for pearls. My lover's words
    were shooting stars which fell to earth as kisses
    on these lips; my body now a softer rhyme
    to his, now echo, assonance; his touch
    a verb dancing in the centre of a noun.
10 Some nights, I dreamed he'd written me, the bed
    a page beneath his writer's hands. Romance
    and drama played by touch, by scent, by taste.
    In the other bed, the best, our guests dozed on,
    dribbling their prose. My living laughing love –
15 I hold him in the casket of my widow's head
    as he held me upon that next best bed.

Questions

40. The poem deals with the relationship between Anne Hathaway and her husband, William Shakespeare.
Summarise what the relationship was like according to the poem.

2

41. Show how **two** examples of the poet's use of language in lines 3–5 of the poem help to clarify the importance of the bed.

4

42. Show how any **two** examples of the poet's use of language in lines 5–11 – 'My lover's words…his writer's hands' – effectively contribute to the main ideas or concerns of the poem.

4

43. How effective do you find any aspect of the closing lines – 'My living…best bed' – as a conclusion to the poem?
Your answer might deal with ideas and/or language.

2

44. With close textual reference, show how the ideas and/or language of this poem are similar OR different to another poem or poems by Carol Ann Duffy that you have read.

8

If you choose to write on this text in Section A you may not write a critical essay on poetry in Section B.

Read the poem below and then attempt the following questions.

Text 2

***Bed* by Jackie Kay**

She is that guid tae me so she is
an Am a burden tae her, I know Am ur.
Stuck here in this blastit bed
year in, year oot, ony saint wuid complain.

5   There's things she has tae dae fir me
A' wish she didnae huv tae dae.
Am her wean noo, wey ma great tent o' nappy,
an champed egg in a cup, an mashed tattie.

Aw the treats A' used tae gie her,
10 she's gieing me. A' dinny ken whit happened.
We dinny talk any mair. Whether it's jist
the blethers ha been plucked oot o' us

an Am here like some skinny chicken,
ma skin aw bubbles and dots and spots,
15 loose flap noo (an yet as a young wuman
A' took pride in ma guid smooth skin.)

Aw A' dae is sit an look oot this windae.
A've seen hale generations graw up
an simmer doon fray this same windae –
20 that's no seen a lick o' paint fir donkeys.

The Kerrs have disappeared, but the last
Campbells ur still here so Am telt –
tho' hauf the time A' dinny believe her:
A've no seen ony Campbell in a long time.

25 My dochter says 'Awright mother?'
haunds me a thin broth or puried neep
an A say 'Aye fine,' an canny help
the great heaving sigh that comes oot

my auld looselips, nor ma crabbit tut,
30 nor ma froon when A' pu' ma cardie tight
aroon ma shooders fir the night drawn in.
Am jist biding time so am ur.

Time is whit A' hauld between
the soft bits o' ma thumbs,
35 the skeleton underneath ma night goon;
aw the while the glaring selfish moon

lights up this drab wee prison.
A'll be gone and how wull she feel?
No that Am saying A' want her guilty.
40 No that Am saying Am no grateful.

Questions

45. The poem deals with the effects of illness and ageing.

    (a) Identify **two** of the problems that are mentioned in the first three stanzas.   **2**

    (b) Show how **two** examples of the poet's use of language in these stanzas help to convey these problems to the reader.   **4**

46. Show how any **two** examples of the poet's use of language from stanzas 4–8 effectively contribute to the main ideas or concerns of the poem.   **4**

47. How effective do you find any aspect of the final two stanzas as a conclusion to the poem?
Your answer might deal with ideas and/or language.   **2**

48. With close textual reference, show how the ideas and/or language of this poem are similar OR different to another poem or poems by Jackie Kay that you have read.   **8**

If you choose to write on this text in Section A you may not write a critical essay on poetry in Section B.

Read the poem below and then attempt the following questions.

Text 3

***Sounds of the Day* by Norman MacCaig**

When a clatter came,

It was horses crossing the ford.

When the air creaked, it was

A lapwing seeing us off the premises

5   Of its private marsh. A snuffling puff

Ten yards from the boat was the tide blocking,

Unblocking a hole in a rock.

When the black drums rolled, it was water

Falling sixty feet into itself.

10   When the door

Scraped shut, it was the end

Of all the sounds there are.

You left me

Beside the quietest fire in the world.

15   I thought I was hurt in my pride only,

Forgetting that,

When you plunge your hand in freezing water,

You feel

A bangle of ice around your wrist

20   Before the whole hand goes numb.

Questions

49. The first stanza describes the 'sounds' of the title.

    (a) **In your own words**, explain what **two** of these sounds are.

    2

    (b) Referring closely to the text, comment on the effectiveness of any **two** of these descriptions.

    4

50. Show how the poet's use of contrast in lines 10–14 effectively contributes to the main ideas of the poem.

    4

51. How effective do you find the language of the final stanza as a conclusion to the poem?

    2

52. With close textual reference, show how the ideas and/or language of this poem are similar OR different to another poem or poems by Norman MacCaig that you have read

    8

If you choose to write on this text in Section A you may not write a critical essay on poetry in Section B.

Read the poem below and then attempt the following questions.

Text 4

Hyena by Edwin Morgan

I am waiting for you.

I have been travelling all morning through the bush

And not eaten.

I am lying at the edge of the bush

5 On a dusty path that leads from the burnt-out kraal.

I am panting, it is midday, I found no water-hole.

I am very fierce without food and although my eyes

Are screwed to slits against the sun

You must believe I am prepared to spring.

10 What do you think of me?

I have a rough coat like Africa.

I am crafty with dark spots

Like the bush-tufted plains of Africa.

I sprawl as a shaggy bundle of gathered energy

15 Like Africa sprawling in its waters.

I trot, I lope, I slaver, I am a ranger.

I hunch my shoulders. I eat the dead.

Do you like my song?

When the moon pours hard and cold on the veldt

20 I sing, and I am the slave of darkness.

Over the stone walls and the mud walls and the ruined places

And the owls, the moonlight falls.

I sniff a broken drum. I bristle. My pelt is silver.

I howl my song to the moon – up it goes.

25   Would you meet me there in the waste places?

It is said I am a good match

For a dead lion. I put my muzzle

At his golden flanks, and tear. He

Is my golden supper, but my tastes are easy.

30   I have a crowd of fangs, and I use them.

Oh and my tongue – do you like me

When it comes lolling out over my jaw

Very long, and I am laughing?

I am not laughing.

35   But I am not snarling either, only

Panting in the sun, showing you

What I grip

Carrion with.

I am waiting

40   For the foot to slide,

For the heart to seize,

For the leaping sinews to go slack,

For the fight to the death to be fought to the death,

For a glazing eye and a rumour of blood.

45   I am crouching in my dry shadows

Till you are ready for me.

My place is to pick you clean

And leave your bones to the wind.

Questions

53. Morgan describes the hyena in the first two stanzas.

    (a) Identify **two** characteristics of the hyena in these stanzas.

        2

    (b) Show how **two** examples of the poet's use of language in the first two stanzas helps to clarify or illustrate his meaning.

        4

54. Show how any **two** examples of the poet's use of language in stanzas 3 and/or 4 effectively contribute to the main ideas or concerns of the poem.

    4

55. How effective do you find any aspect of the final stanza as a conclusion to the poem?

    Your answer might deal with ideas and/or language.

    2

56. With close textual reference, show how the ideas and/or language of this poem are similar OR different to another poem or poems by Edwin Morgan that you have read.

    8

Section B — Critical Essay — 20 marks

Write a critical essay on **one** question from this section of the exam paper. Select your question from **one** of the genres.

You can write on a Scottish text but **not** the same text you answered on in Section A of the exam. You must also write on a different **genre** to the one you selected in Section A.

You have approximately 45 minutes to complete your critical essay.

DRAMA

Answers to questions in this part should refer to the text and to such relevant features as characterisation, key scene(s), structure, climax, theme, plot, conflict, setting…

1. Choose a play that builds to a climax.

   Describe how the playwright builds up to the climax and then, by referring to appropriate techniques, go on to explain why the climax is vital to the play as a whole.

2. Choose a play where your attitude to the main character changes as the play progresses.

   By referring to appropriate techniques, show how the character's nature is portrayed, then go on to show how our attitude changes towards her/him.

PROSE

Answers to questions in this part should refer to the text and to such relevant features as characterisation, setting, language, key incident(s), climax, turning point, plot, structure, narrative technique, theme, ideas, description…

3. Choose a novel or short story or a work of non-fiction in which setting in time and/or place is an important feature.

   By referring to appropriate techniques, show how the author has portrayed this setting and how this influenced your response to the text.

4. Choose a novel or short story which presents a theme that is relevant to you.
   By referring to appropriate techniques, show how the author has explored this theme.

POETRY

Answers to questions in this part should refer to the text and to such relevant features as word choice, tone, imagery, structure, content, rhythm, rhyme, theme, sound, ideas...

5. Choose a poem that deals with the passing of time.

   Describe how the use of poetic techniques helps you to appreciate the treatment of this theme.

6. Choose a poem that creates a strong emotional response.

   Explain briefly what the poem is about, then – by referring to appropriate techniques – show how the poem creates this response in the reader.

FILM and TV DRAMA*

Answers to questions in this part should refer to the text and to such relevant features as use of camera, key sequence, characterisation, mise-en-scène, editing, setting, music/sound, special effects, plot, dialogue...

7. Choose a film or TV drama that has an attention-grabbing opening sequence.

   By referring to appropriate techniques, explain how the film or television makers have made the opening sequence effective.

8. Choose a film or TV drama that deals with the dark side of society or human nature.

   By referring to appropriate techniques, explain how the film or television makers have dealt with this theme.

* 'TV drama' includes a single play, a series or a serial.

LANGUAGE STUDY

Answers to questions in this part should refer to the text and to such relevant features as register, accent, dialect, slang, jargon, vocabulary, tone, abbreviation...

9. Choose a method of communication such as email or text messaging.

   By referring to specific examples from your chosen text, show the features of language used in this method of communication and discuss the advantages and disadvantages of this method.

10. Consider adverts for a particular product such as perfume, cars or any other product.

By referring to specific features of language use, show how the advert attempts to persuade its audience.

[END OF QUESTION PAPER]

Practice Exam B

N5

Practice Papers for SQA Exams

ENGLISH

NATIONAL 5

Exam B

Reading for Understanding, Analysis and Evaluation

Date — Not applicable

Duration — 1 hour

Total marks: 30

Read the extract and then answer the questions in your own words as much as possible. Try to answer all of the questions.

Scotland's leading educational publishers

Can an ape learn to be human?

In this article from The Independent, Steve Connor examines the intelligence of humans' closest relatives, chimpanzees.

Many years ago while on a visit to London Zoo I experienced first-hand the wily intelligence of chimpanzees in the days when they were kept behind wire mesh. The captive troupe had rehearsed a kind of primate nonchalance that would attract a curious crowd of onlookers gathered around their caged compound. Then, with little warning, they would start to fling
5   dung at their human audience, jumping up and down with apparent glee at the sight of the fleeing crowd.

As dirty protests go, it was relatively unsophisticated. Some years later, primatologist Mathias Osvath of Lund University in Sweden documented a rather more complex strand of protest in a chimp called Santino who lives in Furuvik Zoo. Santino showed that it was possible for
10   chimps to plan for the future. He did this by methodically building up a cache of stones in the early morning, hours before opening time. When the first zoo visitors appeared, he began to enthusiastically hurl his missiles at the gawping humans.

Dr Osvath concluded that Santino's actions showed that chimps have a rather well developed form of intelligence. By anticipating opening time, and preparing for it with his cache of rocks,
15   Santino and the dung-chucking chimps at London Zoo were able to construct mental pictures of the future using forward planning.

The degree to which chimps think and behave like humans has been the subject of endless speculation, and many scientific studies. When we gaze into the face of the chimpanzee, Pan troglodytes, our closest living relative with whom we share more than 98 per cent of our DNA, we
20   are also looking into the eyes of another highly sentient being who might in many ways pass for one of us.

Indeed, chimps are capable of an array of behaviours that were once considered the sole preserve of humans and some scientists have seriously suggested that chimps, which belong to the genus Pan, should in fact be classified as Homo – the human family. They make simple tools, they are
25   fascinated by fire and rain and have even been known to appreciate a sunset. They mourn their dead, they make war on members of the same species and, rather chillingly, they are said to be the only animal other than humans who deliberately plan the murder of rivals.

They are also capable of endearing acts of love and tenderness. They actively seek one another's affections and reassurance, they can laugh and be tickled, they conspire with one another
30   and form alliances. They are able to recognise themselves in a mirror, are capable of 'tactical deception' to fool a companion or competitor, and they even show signs of engaging in the kind of rudimentary fictional play behaviour seen in very young children.

Chimpanzees are considered to be the most intelligent of all the 'non-human' primates, which include the other apes such as the gorilla and orang-utan. But their intelligence is both
35   fascinating and frightening, in part because there is something irrevocably inhuman about the adult chimp's bestial strength and unpredictability.

Juvenile chimps can be very sweet but they grow into formidable beefcakes with a body strength several times greater than the strongest man. Yet they have the temperament of a two-year-old, as Charla Nash, a 55-year-old woman from Connecticut, can testify. In 2009, she had her face
40 ripped off by a 200lb pet chimpanzee called Travis who up to that moment had been the adored companion of Nash's best friend.

The film, *Rise of the Planet of the Apes*, plays on this fear. In it, the innate strength and agility of chimps is powerfully combined with a kind of artificial, supercharged intelligence accidentally conferred to the primates by an experiment gone wrong. Scientists searching for a cure for
45 Alzheimer's infect a chimp called Caesar with a potential new treatment, which involves the growth of new brain cells that coincidentally impart a human-like intelligence. In the film the lead character Caesar learns to communicate with his human captors with sign language, having mastered some 300 individual signs.

This is not such a fanciful concept. Experiments where chimps have been trained to learn a sign
50 language are well-established. Washoe, a chimp who in the 1960s was captured in the wild as a baby in West Africa, was the first primate to learn American Sign Language. He was raised as a human child in Washoe County, Nevada, by a pair of husband-and-wife psychologists who taught him several hundred signs. Apparently, when Washoe first saw a swan he made the signs for 'water' and 'bird', which led one Harvard psychologist to say that it was like 'getting an SOS from
55 outer space'.

More elaborate experiments involving the use of mirrors have demonstrated that chimps are better than any other intelligent animal at recognising their own reflections. This is considered important because being self-aware provides a capacity to reflect on internal mental states – as René Descartes pointed out: 'I think, therefore I am.'

60 However, chimps are far from having the sort of intelligence we equate with a normal human child. This is hardly surprising given that the human brain is about three times larger in comparison to body size compared to the chimp brain. We last shared a common ancestor with each other between 5 and 7 million years ago. Some 350,000 generations separate our evolutionary history, a long period of genetic partition that explains why we are intellectually
65 so different.

And yet, studies of wild chimps living in their natural forest habitats of West Africa show a surprising similarity of behaviours. They routinely make simple tools, for example stripping thin branches of their leaves to fish for termites or using leaves as sponges for drinking. They also pass on their technological know-how to the next generation.

70 In the wild, the common chimp lives in a society dominated by an 'alpha male', but he can only rule if he is able to enrol the help of a band of 'beta males' using skillful, almost Machiavellian guile. Indeed, primatologists observing chimps in the wild and in captivity have documented many instances of 'tactical deception', when one chimp tries to deceive another, whether it is pretending not to notice a banana for fear that others may see you with it, or trying to covertly
75 mate behind the back of the alpha male.

It is this kind of Machiavellian intelligence that we humans are so good at. We have our good side, but we also lie and cheat in order to gain advantage over others. Studies of chimps suggest that this type of behaviour may go back to our shared common ancestor. When we watch chimps and how they treat one another, we are seeing how our own direct ancestors

80 may have behaved many millions of years ago. In other words, there is a little bit of troglodyte in all of us. That's what we find so unnerving when we look into the eyes of our closest living relative.

Can an ape learn to be human? by Steve Connor. Published in *The Independent*, Friday 5 August 2011.

Questions

1. (a) Look at lines 1–16. **In your own words**, explain how the chimps in these examples showed signs of intelligence.

    4

    (b) Explain how the writer's word choice in these lines helps to emphasise this intelligence.

    4

2. Look at lines 17–32. **In your own words**, explain what similarities the writer points out between chimpanzees and humans.

    4

3. Look at lines 33–41. **In your own words**, explain the factors that make chimpanzees 'frightening'.

    3

4. **In your own words**, explain what has been achieved in the experiments in teaching language to the chimp, Washoe. Refer to lines 49–55.

    2

5. Look at lines 60–65. **In your own words**, how does the writer explain why humans are 'intellectually so different' to chimpanzees?

    2

6. Look at lines 66–75. **In your own words**, explain **one** of the types of behaviour displayed by chimpanzees and discuss why it shows similar behaviour to humans.

    2

7. Read the last paragraph. Identify how the writer thinks that considering chimpanzees can make us feel. Give evidence to support your answer.

    2

8. Choose **one** of the following images:
    *   'chimps at London Zoo were able to construct mental pictures of the future'
    *   'they grow into formidable beefcakes'
    *   'when Washoe first saw a swan he made the signs for "water" and "bird", which…was like "getting an SOS from outer space".

    Explain what your chosen image means and analyse its effect.

    3

9. Referring to the whole article, **in your own words** summarise the key points the writer makes about chimpanzees.

    4

[END OF QUESTION PAPER]

Practice Papers for SQA Exams

ENGLISH
NATIONAL 5
Exam B
Critical Reading

Date — Not applicable

Duration — 1 hour and 30 minutes

Total marks: 40

Section A: Scottish Text – 20 marks

Choose an extract from a Scottish text you have studied and then answer the questions. Try to complete all of the questions.

Choose only **one** text from either Part A Drama, Part B Prose or Part C Poetry.

Section B: Critical Essay – 20 marks

Write **one** critical essay on a text you have studied from one of the genres of Drama, Prose, Poetry, Film and TV Drama or Language Study.

You are permitted to write an essay on a text from the list of Scottish texts, providing that you have not written about the same text in Section A and that the genre you select is not the same as the one you answered on in Section A.

Each section of the exam should take approximately 45 minutes to complete.

Section A — Scottish Text — 20 marks

Answer the questions from **one** of the three sections only (Drama, Prose or Poetry).

Read the text carefully and then answer **all** of the questions on the text, writing the answers in your own words as much as possible.

SCOTTISH TEXT (DRAMA)

If you choose to write on this text in Section A you may not write a critical essay on drama in Section B.

Read the extract below and then attempt the following questions.

Text 1

Bold Girls by Rona Munro

CASSIE: Oh my daddy was a lovely man. Gentle. He'd hold you in his lap like you had fur and he didn't want to ruffle it. He held me like that anyway. There's been men that've told me I'm pretty and men that've told me I'm clever and men that've sworn I'm some kind of angel come down to pull them out of a sea of whisky and
5   give them the kiss of life. (*Pause*) Lying hounds every one of them. (*Pause*) My daddy said that I was the best girl that ever stirred her daddy's tea for him. The best girl that ever sat on his lap or combed his hair or did any of the wee things he wasn't fit to do for himself. My daddy said I was special. (*Pause*) My daddy never lied to me. So it must have been me that lied to him.

10   *Cassie exits*

               Lights revert to normal

               Marie is slowly tidying up and shredding bread for the birds

MARIE: I like the pigeons. I saw a pigeon fly across the sky and when it crossed the clouds it was black but when it flew past the roofs it was white. It could fly as far as it
15   liked but it never went further than Turf Lodge from what I could see. (*Pause*) I used to watch for that bird, the only white bird that wasn't a seagull. (*Pause*) He wasn't even the man they wanted, but they shot him; that made him the man they wanted. (*Pause*) You have to imagine the four of them. All men you'd look at twice one way or another. Michael, my husband, because he had that strong feel to him.
20   You felt it in the back of your neck when he came into the room. People turned to look without knowing why. Davey, my brother now, you'd look again but you'd say, what's that wee boy doing in his daddy's jacket. Nineteen and he looks more like nine, though they've put age in his eyes for him now. He's got old eyes now. Martin, Cassie's brother, you'd look and you'd cross the street in case he caught
25   your eye and decided he didn't like the look of *you*, he's got the kind of eyebrows that chop short conversations, slamming a glower on his face like two fists hitting a table – and Joe, Cassie's husband. You'd look at him to see what the joke was, Joe's always laughing, Joe's always where the crack is. (*Pause*) Davey's in the Kesh.

30

Martin's in the Kesh. Joe's in the Kesh – and Michael is dead. (*Pause*) They didn't really go around together, the four of them, just every odd Saturday they'd be in here playing cards till they were three of them broke and Joe stuffed with beer and winning. Singing till they were too drunk to remember the words then waking and eating and drinking some more till they were drunk enough to make up their own. Sure it was a party they had. And Davey felt like a man and

35

Martin smiled and Joe sang almost in tune and Michael would tell me he loved me over and over till he'd made a song out of that. (*Pause*) Sometimes he said he loved me when he'd no drink in him at all. Sometimes he even did that.

Marie finishes tidying and exits.

Questions

1. How does Cassie's language express her feelings about:

    (a) her father

    2

    (b) the other men she has known

    4

2. With close reference to the text, explain how the playwright reveals Marie's impression of:

    (a) the men as a group

    2

    (b) **two** of the men that she describes in her speech

    4

3. The extract shows the influence of men on the women in the play. With close reference to the rest of the play, explain how the theme of gender is explored.

    8

If you choose to write on this text in Section A you may not write a critical essay on drama in Section B.

Read the extract below and then attempt the following questions.

Text 2

***Tally's Blood* by Anne-Marie di Mambro**

	MASSIMO:	It's time we talked about Hughie –
	ROSINELLA:	(*Interrupting*) Take me to Italy, Massimo.
	MASSIMO:	What?
	ROSINELLA:	I want to go to Italy.
5	MASSIMO:	Why – all of a sudden?
	ROSINELLA:	Just to get away from here.
	MASSIMO:	But why now?
	ROSINELLA:	Because I can't face it here. There's too much heartache.
	MASSIMO:	How long for?
10	ROSINELLA:	I don't care.
	MASSIMO:	What about the shop?
	ROSINELLA:	Do what you like with it. Shut it. Sell it. I don't care if we never come back.

Massimo looks at her with disbelief.

	MASSIMO:	You mean that, don't you?
15	ROSINELLA:	I just want away.
	MASSIMO:	When I think of the times I've asked you to come to Italy with me. Oh, but you always had an excuse ready. Now – because YOU'RE unhappy, because YOU miss Lucia – we've just to go. Just like that. To hell with the shop, to hell with everything I've worked for. To hell with everything except what YOU want.
20	ROSINELLA;	If you knew what I've been through.
	MASSIMO:	Oh Rosie, Rosie, do you think I don't know? 'What you've been through'. It's all I've ever heard. But what about the rest of us? Do we not go through anything? What about Lucia – what about Hughie – what about me?
	ROSINELLA:	Massimo…please. Don't do this to me.
25	MASSIMO:	But you really don't care for anyone else's pain except your own, do you? I never realised that before and I wish to God I didn't now. All these years, I've known what it meant to you, no being able to have a family. God knows, you never tried to hide

MARKS
Do not write in this margin

30

it. Never. But did you ever once think what it's been like for me? Did you ever think maybe I would have liked a child? A son to work alongside me, to plan things with. A son to leave my shop to… You know something else, Rosinella? It's only now I know what I must've put my own father through. *(Voice breaks)* But you! You never think of anyone but yourself.

He goes; Rosinella shattered: Hughie in, doesn't see him at first. She turns and looks at him, very sadly.

Questions

4. **In your own words**, summarise the conflict between Massimo and Rosinella. Make at least **four** key points.

4

5. With close reference to the text, explain how the playwright reveals Rosinella's emotions in this extract.

4

6. With close reference to the text, explain how the playwright reveals Massimo's reaction to Rosinella's request.

4

7. By referring to this extract, and to at least **two** other incidents from elsewhere in the play, explain how the character of Rosinella changes and develops as the play progresses.

8

If you choose to write on this text in Section A you may not write a critical essay on drama in Section B.

Read the extract below and then attempt the following questions.

Text 3

***Sailmaker* by Alan Spence**

This extract comes from the opening of the play.

Act One

Dark. Light on ALEC, centre stage.

ALEC: Sometimes I wake up in the middle of the night and I can remember it. The feeling.

I was only a boy. Eleven.

5   There was this knock at the door. The middle of the night.

Batter. Batter.

It was a policeman. He said my mother had taken a turn for the worse. My father had to go down to the hospital.

I couldn't get back to sleep.

10   It was getting light by the time he came back.

(Lights fade up. DAVIE enters, stands behind ALEC)

DAVIE: Ah've got a bit of bad news for ye son. Yer mammy's dead.

ALEC: Part of me already knew, accepted it. Part of me couldn't. Part of me cried.

DAVIE: Ah've got a bit of bad news for ye son.

15 ALEC: I cried and a numbness came over me, shielding me from the real pain.

DAVIE: Yer mammy's dead.

ALEC: I was standing there, crying – real big deep sobs. But the other part of me, the part of me that accepted, was just watching.

DAVIE: Yer mammy's dead.

20 ALEC: I was watching myself crying, watching my puny grief from somewhere above it all. I was me and I was not-me.

DAVIE: Yer mammy's dead.

(ALEC turns to face him)

There's just you an me now son. We'll have tae make the best of it.

25   Ah'll make some breakfast.

ALEC: Ah'm no really very hungry.

DAVIE:		Naw. Ah'll make a cuppa tea.

(Moves back, quietly busies himself, sets fire in the hearth)

ALEC:
30

Later on I opened the window and looked out across the back courts. The breeze was warm. Everything was the same. It was very ordinary. Nothing had changed. I don't know what I had expected. A sign. Jesus to come walking across the back and tell me everything was all right. A window in the sky to open and God to lean out and say my mother had arrived safe. The sun shone on the grey tenements, on the railings and the middens, on the dustbins and the spilled

35

ashes. It glinted on windows and on bits of broken glass. It was like something I remembered, something from a dream. Across the back, a wee boy was standing, blowing on a mouth-organ, playing the same two notes over and over again.

(Two notes on mouth organ, repeated, continuing while he talks)

My mother was dead.

40

My mother was dead.

The breeze touched my cheek. It scattered the ashes round the midden. It ruffled the clothes of the wee boy standing there, playing his two notes.

Over and over and over.

I looked up at the sky, the clouds moving across. Just for a minute a gap opened

45

up, a wee patch of clear blue.

(Two notes continuing, then fade)

DAVIE:

We better get this place tidied up a bit son. Folk'll be comin back after the funeral.

(Moves around as he is talking – ALEC remains static)

As long as ye keep movin it doesnae hit ye. Get the fire goin clean the windaes

50

dust the furniture hink about something for eating don't stop keep yerself goin. Sometimes for whole minutes ye can nearly *nearly* forget about it, shove it tae the back ae yer mind. Then maybe yer lookin for something and ye turn round tae ask her where it as an ye wonder for a minute where she's got tae and ye think she's through in the room an ye catch yerself thinkin it and it hits ye an ye think Christ

55

this is it this is me for the rest ae ma days.

Questions

8. **In your own words**, summarise the way that Alec and Davie experience grief in this extract. Make at least **four** key points.

4

9. Look at lines 2–24. Show how the writer's use of language helps to make this an effective opening to the play.

4

10. Look at lines 24–57. Show how the writer's language clarifies the impact of grief on:

(a) Davie

2

(b) Alec

2

11. Alec is the central character in the play.

With close reference to the rest of the play, explain how the character of Alec develops.

8

SCOTTISH TEXT (PROSE)

If you choose to write on this text in Section A you may not write a critical essay on prose in Section B.

Read the extract below and then attempt the following questions.

Text 1

The Telegram **by Iain Crichton Smith**

The two women who watched the street were different, not only physically but socially. For the thin woman's son was a sub-lieutenant in the Navy while the fat woman's son was an ordinary seaman. The fat woman's son had to salute the thin woman's son. One got more pay than the other, and wore better uniform. One had been at university and had therefore
5 become an officer, the other had left school at the age of fourteen.

When they looked out of the window they could see cows lazing about, but little other movement. The fat woman's cow used to eat the thin woman's washing and she was looking out for it but she couldn't see it. The thin woman was not popular in the village. She was an incomer from another village and had only been in this one for thirty years or so. The fat woman had lived
10 in the village all her days; she was a native. Also the thin woman was ambitious: she had sent her son to university though she only had a widow's pension of ten shillings a week.

As they watched they could see at the far end of the street the tall man in black clothes carrying in his hand a piece of yellow paper. This was a bare village with little colour and therefore the yellow was both strange and unnatural.

15 'The fat woman said: 'It's Macleod again.'

'I wonder where he's going today.'

They were both frightened for he could be coming to their house. And so they watched him and as they watched him they spoke feverishly as if by speaking continually and watching his every move they would be able to keep from themselves whatever plague he was bringing. The thin
20 woman said:

'Don't worry, Sarah, it won't be for you. Donald only left last week.'

'You don't know,' said the fat woman, 'you don't know.' And then she added without thinking, 'It's different for the officers.'

'Why is it different for the officers?' said the thin woman in an even voice without taking her eyes
25 from the black figure.

'Well, I just thought they'd be better off,' said the fat woman in a confused tone, 'they get better food and they get better conditions.'

'They're still on the ship,' said the thin woman who was thinking that the fat woman was very stupid. But then most of them were: they were large, fat and lazy. Most of them could have better
30 afforded to send their sons and daughters to university but they didn't want to be thought of as snobbish.

'They are that,' said the fat woman. 'But your son is educated,' she added irrelevantly. Of course her son didn't salute the thin woman's son if they were both home on leave at the same time. It had happened once they had been. But naturally there was the uneasiness.

35   'I made sacrifices to have my son educated,' said the thin woman. 'I lived on a pension of ten shillings a week. I was in nobody's debt. More tea?'

'No thank you,' said the fat woman. 'He's passed Bessie's house. That means it can't be Roddy. He's safe.'

For a terrible moment she realised that she hoped that the elder would have turned in at Bessie's
40   house. Not that she had anything against Bessie or Roddy. But still one thought of one's own family first.

The thin woman continued remorselessly as if she were pecking away at something she had pecked at for many years. 'The teacher told me to send Iain to University. He came to see me. I had no thought of sending him before he came.'

45   '"Send your son to University," he said to me. "He's got a good head on him." And I'll tell you, Sarah, I had to save every penny. Ten shillings isn't much. When did you see me with good clothes in the church?'

The thin woman continued: 'Many's the night I used to sit here in this room and knit clothes for him when he was young. I even knitted trousers for him. And for all I know he may marry an
50   English girl and where will I be? He might go and work in England. He was staying in a house there at Christmas. He met a girl at a dance and he found out later that her father was a mayor. I'm sure she smokes and drinks. And he might not give me anything after all I've done for him.'

'Donald spends all his money,' said the fat woman. 'He never sends me anything. When he comes home on leave he's never in the house. But I don't mind. He was always like that. Meeting
55   strange people and buying them drinks. It's his nature and he can't go against his nature. He's passed the Smiths. That means Tommy's all right.'

There were only another three houses before he would reach her own, and then the last one was the one where she was sitting.

Questions

12. Look at lines 1–11. The two women are different 'not only physically but socially.' **In your own words**, summarise the differences between the two women.

4

13. Look at lines 12–27. Show how the writer's use of language contributes to the growing tension.

2

14. Look at lines 28–31. How does the thin woman feel at this point and how does the writer's use of language make this clear?

2

15. Look at lines 35–58. The **two** women reflect on the difficulties of their relationships with their sons. Explain how **two** examples of the writer's use of language convey these difficulties.

4

16. By referring to this extract and the story *The Telegram* as a whole, explain how the ideas/language are similar OR different to at least **one** other story by Iain Crichton Smith that you have read.

8

If you choose to write on this text in Section A you may not write a critical essay on prose in Section B.

Read the extract below and then attempt the following questions.

Text 2

***Zimmerobics* by Anne Donovan**

In this extract, the narrator, Miss Knight, is persuaded by the instructor, Cheryl, to take her first exercise class in the old folks' home.

'So now I'm targeting older people. If it's a success, I'm hoping to get a business grant. There's lots of old folks' homes looking for something like this for their residents. I really want to make a video and sell it so that all up and down the country there are senior citizens doing Zimmerobics with Cheryl.'

5   'Well, dear, that sounds very nice. I hope you're successful.'

'So I'll see you on Thursday then? Eleven o'clock.'

'I'll think about it.'

That's what I always say when I've no intention of doing something but, over the weekend, I kept thinking about it. I'd seen aerobics on the TV once when I'd lost the remote control
10 and couldn't switch the thing off; impossibly shaped women in shiny skin-tight clothes doing things with their bodies I didn't know bodies did. The idea of Cheryl teaching that sort of thing to us; humph-backit, shuffling behind metal frames with our swollen feet, well, it didn't bear thinking about. There was something about the girl, though, her enthusiasm about the project, that attracted me. I've always been attracted by enthusiasts, not being one myself.

15 So that was that. At 11am I assembled with the others in the dayroom. I knew most of their faces, but was surprised to see some of them wearing tracksuits and trainers. It hadn't occurred to me to ask what to wear and I didn't possess such things anyway, but somehow I felt out of place. It was like starting school and discovering that the others were wearing school uniform and you weren't.

20 Cheryl bounced into the room, wearing a pair of trainers that made her feet like a horse's hooves. Her hair was tied back with an emerald green band which matched her shimmering leotard and tights.

'I hope she doesn't need to go to the toilet in a hurry,' muttered a voice behind me.

'Hi there. It's great to see so many of you here this morning. Now, take it at your own pace and if
25 you feel uncomfortable or out of breath at any time, stop for a wee rest. Enjoy!'

She switched on the music. We stood behind our Zimmers as she got us to stretch first one, then the other, arm, move our heads to each side, then stretch our legs. I heard a few creaking sounds but so far so good. We moved on to circling movements and, as the record progressed, I felt an unaccustomed but pleasant tingling in my limbs.

30 'That was the warm-up. The next one's a bit faster.'

The next record was a catchy tune about living in the YMCA. I couldn't keep up with the routine at first but, once we'd been through it a few times, I became quite proficient. We had to raise our right then our left arms to the Y and the M, then pause on the C and hold our Zimmers as we bent both legs for the A. Then we marched (well, shuffled in most cases) round
35 to the left, raised our arms twice to the Y and the M (that was a bit tricky), paused at the C and kicked our left leg to the A. During the verse we did some marching and a few kicks, then we repeated the chorus routine, this time moving to the right. At the end we clapped three times, boldly taking both hands off our Zimmer frames.

It was brilliant. I hadn't felt like this for years. My body was old and decrepit, but it still worked.
40 I had been concentrating so hard on what I was doing I had forgotten the others, but now I looked round and saw their faces, flushed and smiling.

'You all did great. Give yourselves a round of applause.' She clapped her hands above her head while we patted our hands together, slightly embarrassed.

'Same time next week,' she called as we hirpled out of the dayroom, old once again.

45 The memory of the exercise class lingered on for the rest of the day, not just in my mind as I relived the routine, but in my bones and muscles. I thought I'd be sore and stiff but, surprisingly, I felt better, as though someone had oiled all the creaky old joints. There was a feeling in them which I suppose you could call an ache, but it was a pleasant ache, an ache of life.

Questions

17. Summarise what happens in this extract from the short story. Make at least **four** key points. 4

18. Look at lines 1–6. What is Cheryl like and how does the writer use language to convey the character of Cheryl? 2

19. Look at lines 7–19. What are Mrs Knight's feelings about the class before it begins and how does the writer's use of language make this clear? 2

20. Look at lines 26–48. Show how any **two** examples of the writer's use of language contribute to Miss Knight's growing enthusiasm about her Zimmerobics class. 4

21. By referring to this extract and the story *Zimmerobics* as a whole, explain how the ideas/language are similar OR different to at least **one** other story by Anne Donovan that you have read. 8

If you choose to write on this text in Section A you may not write a critical essay on prose in Section B.

Read the extract below and then attempt the following questions.

Text 3

***The Testament of Gideon Mack* by James Robertson**

In this extract Gideon reflects upon his childhood and the influence of his upbringing.

When I was a child I spoke as a child, I understood as a child, I thought as a child: yet I was already, in so many ways, the man I would become. I think back on how cold I was, even then. It is hard to recall, not that I burn with this dry, feverish fire, but cold I certainly was. There was ice built around my heart, years of it. How could it have been otherwise? The manse at
5 Ochtermill saw to that.

I have walked and run through this world pretending emotions rather than feeling them. Oh, I could feel pain, physical pain, but I had to imagine joy, sorrow, anger. As for love, I didn't know what it meant. But I learned early to keep myself well disguised. To the world at large I was just Gideon Mack, a dutiful wee boy growing in the shadow of his father and of the Kirk.

10 As that wee boy I was taught that, solitary though I might be, I was never alone. Always there was one who walked beside me. I could not see him, but he was there, constant at my side. I wanted to know him, to love and be loved by him, but he did not reveal himself. He frightened me. I had neither the courage to reject him nor the capacity to embrace him.

This is the hard lesson of my life: love is not in us from the beginning, like an instinct; love is no
15 more original to human beings than sin. Like sin, it has to be learned.

Then I put away childish things, and for years I thought I saw with the clarity of reason. I did not believe in anything I could not see. I mocked at shadows and sprites. That constant companion was not there at all: I did not believe in him, and he did not reveal himself to me. Yet, through circumstance and through choice, I was to become his servant, a minister of religion. How ironic
20 this is, and yet how natural, as if the path were laid out for me from birth, and though I wandered a little from it, distracted or deluded here and there, yet I was always bound to return to it again.

And all the while this fire was burning deep inside me. I kept it battened down, the door of the furnace tightly shut, because that seemed necessary in order to get through life. I never savoured life for what it was: I only wanted to get to the next stage of it. I wish now I'd taken a little more
25 time, but it is too late for such regrets. I was like the child in the cinema whose chief anticipation lies not in the film but in wondering what he will do after it is over; I was the reader who hurries through a 500-page novel not to see what will happen but simply to get to the end. And now, despite everything, I am there, and for this I must thank that other companion, in who also I did not believe, but who has shown me a way through the shadows and beyond the shadows.

30 I have not preached for weeks, yet I am full of texts. If I am a prophet then I have yet to be heard. If I am Jonah, then the fish has vomited me out but nobody believes where I have been: nobody except the one who saved me from the belly of hell. Who am I? I am Gideon Mack, time-server, charlatan, hypocrite, God's grovelling apologist; the man who saw the Stone, the man that was

35 drowned and that the waters gave back, the mad minister who met with the Devil and lived to tell the tale. And hence my third, non-Scriptural text, for what is religion if not a kind of madness, and what is madness without a touch of religion? And yet there is pace and sanctuary in religion too – it is the asylum to which all poor crazed sinners may come at last, the door which will always open to us if we can only find the courage to knock.

40 Few suspected it, but all my life was a lie from the age of nine (when, through deceit, I almost succeeded in killing my father); all my words were spoken with the tongue of a serpent, and what love I gave or felt came from a dissembling heart. Then I saw the Stone, and nothing was the same again. This is my testimony. Read it and believe it, or believe it not. You may judge me a liar, a cheat, a madman, I do not care. I am beyond questions of probity or sanity now. I am at the gates of the realm of knowledge, and one day soon I will pass through them.

Questions

22. In your own words, summarise **two** of the main points that Gideon makes about his own character in this extract.

2

23. Look at lines 1–15. With close reference to the text, show how the writer creates a clear picture of Gideon as a child. Give **two** examples.

4

24. Look at lines 22–38. Show how any **two** examples of the writer's use of language clarify the character of Gideon.

4

25. Look at the final paragraph. Show how the writer's use of language creates suspense and is effective in making the reader want to read on.

2

26. By referring to this extract, and to at least **two** other incidents from elsewhere in the novel, explain how the writer develops the theme of religion.

8

If you choose to write on this text in Section A you may not write a critical essay on prose in Section B.

Read the extract below and then attempt the following questions.

Text 4

Kidnapped **by Robert Louis Stevenson**

In this extract, David Balfour and Alan Breck are on the run in the Highlands, having been accused of murder.

For all our hurry, day began to come in while we were still far from any shelter. It found us in a prodigious valley, strewn with rocks and where ran a foaming river. Wild mountains stood around it; there grew there neither grass nor trees; and I have sometimes thought since then, that it may have been the valley called Glencoe, where the massacre was in the time of King William.
5 But for the details of our itinerary, I am all to seek; our way lying now by short cuts, now by great detours; our pace being so hurried, our time of journeying usually by night; and the names of such places as I asked and heard being in the Gaelic tongue and the more easily forgotten.

The first peep of morning, then, showed us this horrible place, and I could see Alan knit his brow.

'This is no fit place for you and me,' he said. 'This is a place they're bound to watch.' So there we
10 stood, side by side upon a small rock slippery with spray, a far broader leap in front of us, and the river dinning upon all sides. When I saw where I was, there came on me a deadly sickness of fear, and I put my hand over my eyes. Alan took me and shook me; I saw he was speaking, but the roaring of the falls and the trouble of my mind prevented me from hearing; only I saw his face was red with anger, and that he stamped upon the rock. The same look showed me the water
15 raging by, and the mist hanging in the air: and with that I covered my eyes again and shuddered.

The next minute Alan had set the brandy bottle to my lips, and forced me to drink about a gill, which sent the blood into my head again. Then, putting his hands to his mouth, and his mouth to my ear, he shouted, 'Hang or drown!' and turning his back upon me, leaped over the farther branch of the stream, and landed safe.

20 I was now alone upon the rock, which gave me the more room; the brandy was singing in my ears; I had this good example fresh before me, and just wit enough to see that if I did not leap at once, I should never leap at all. I bent low on my knees and flung myself forth, with that kind of anger of despair that has sometimes stood me in stead of courage. Sure enough, it was but my hands that reached the full length; these slipped, caught again, slipped again; and I was
25 sliddering back into the lynn, when Alan seized me, first by the hair, then by the collar, and with a great strain dragged me into safety.

Never a word he said, but set off running again for his life, and I must stagger to my feet and run after him. I had been weary before, but now I was sick and bruised, and partly drunken with the brandy; I kept stumbling as I ran, I had a stitch that came near to overmaster me; and when at last
30 Alan paused under a great rock that stood there among a number of others, it was none too soon for David Balfour.

A great rock I have said; but by rights it was two rocks leaning together at the top, both some twenty feet high, and at the first sight inaccessible. Even Alan (though you may say he had as good as four hands) failed twice in an attempt to climb them; and it was only at the third trial,
35 and then by standing on my shoulders and leaping up with such force as I thought must have broken my collar-bone, that he secured a lodgment. Once there, he let down his leathern girdle; and with the aid of that and a pair of shallow footholds in the rock, I scrambled up beside him.

Then I saw why we had come there; for the two rocks, being both somewhat hollow on the top and sloping one to the other, made a kind of dish or saucer, where as many as three or four
40 men might have lain hidden.

All this while Alan had not said a word, and had run and climbed with such a savage, silent frenzy of hurry, that I knew that he was in mortal fear of some miscarriage. Even now we were on the rock he said nothing, nor so much as relaxed the frowning look upon his face; but clapped flat down, and keeping only one eye above the edge of our place of shelter scouted
45 all round the compass. The dawn had come quite clear; we could see the stony sides of the valley, and its bottom, which was bestrewed with rocks, and the river, which went from one side to another, and made white falls; but nowhere the smoke of a house, nor any living creature but some eagles screaming round a cliff.

Then at last Alan smiled.

Questions

27. Summarise what happens in this extract from the novel. Make at least **three** key points.　　3

28. Look at lines 1–15. What is the mood or atmosphere created by the writer, and how does the writer use language effectively to create this mood or atmosphere?　　3

29. Look again at lines 16–26. Show how any **two** examples of the writer's use of language contribute to a growing sense of suspense.　　4

30. Look at the final line – 'Then at last Alan smiled.' From what has been described previously in this extract, why is this surprising?　　2

31. By referring to this extract, and to at least **two** other examples from elsewhere in the novel, explain how setting is used in the novel.　　8

If you choose to write on this text in Section A you may not write a critical essay on prose in Section B.

Read the extract below and then attempt the following questions.

Text 5

***The Cone–Gatherers* by Robin Jenkins**

In this extract, from the opening of the novel, Neil and Calum are gathering cones.

It was a good tree by the sea-loch, with many cones and much sunshine; it was homely too, with rests among its topmost branches as comfortable as chairs.

For hours the two men had worked in silence there, a hundred feet from the earth, closer, it seemed, to the blue sky round which they had watched the sun slip. Misted in the morning,
5 the loch had gone through many shades of blue and now was mauve, like the low hills on its far side. Seals that had been playing tag in and out of the seaweed under the surface had disappeared round the point, like children gone home for tea. A destroyer had steamed seawards, with a sailor singing cheerfully. More sudden and swifter than hawks, and roaring louder than waterfalls, aeroplanes had shot down from the wood, whose autumnal colours they seemed
10 to have copied for camouflage, in the silence that had followed gunshots had cracked far off in the wood.

From the tall larch could be glimpsed, across the various-tinted crowns of the trees, the chimneys of the mansion behind its private fence of giant silver firs. Neil, the elder of the brothers, had often paused, his hand stretched out from its ragged sleeve to pluck the sweet resinous cones,
15 and gazed at the great house with a calm yet bitter intentness and anticipation, as if, having put a spell on it, he was waiting for it to change. He never said what he expected or why he watched; nor did his brother ever ask.

For Calum the tree-top was interest enough; in it he was as indigenous as squirrel or bird. His black curly hair was speckled with orange needles; his torn jacket was stained green, as was his
20 left knee visible through a hole rubbed in his trousers. Chaffinches fluttered round him, ignoring his brother; now and then one would alight on his head or shoulder. He kept chuckling to them, and his sunburnt face was alert and beautiful with trust. Yet he was a much faster gatherer than his brother, and reached far out to where the brittle branches drooped and creaked under his weight. Neil would sometimes glance across to call out: 'Careful.' It was the only word spoken in
25 the past two hours.

The time came when, thrilling as a pipe lament across the water, daylight announced it must go: there was a last blaze of light, an uncanny clarity, a splendour and puissance; and then the abdication began. Single stars appeared, glittering in a sky pale and austere. Dusk like a breathing drifted in among the trees and crept over the loch. Slowly the mottled yellow of the chestnuts,
30 the bronze of beech, the saffron of birches, all the magnificent sombre harmonies of decay, became indistinguishable. Owls hooted. A fox barked.

It was past time to climb down and go home. The path to the earth was unfamiliar; in the dark it might be dangerous. Once safely down, they would have to find their way like ghosts to their hut in

the heart of the wood. Yet Neil did not give the word to go down. It was not zeal to fill the bags
35 that made him linger, for he had given up gathering. He just sat, motionless and silent; and his
brother, accustomed to these trances, waited in sympathy: he was sure that even at midnight
he could climb down any tree, and help Neil to climb down too. He did not know what Neil was
thinking, and never asked; even if told he would not understand. It was enough that they were
together.

40 For about half an hour they sat there, no longer working. The scent of the tree seemed to
strengthen with the darkness, until Calum fancied he was resting in the heart of an enormous
flower. As he breathed in the fragrance, he stroked the branches, and to his gentle hands they
were as soft as petals. More owls cried. Listening, as if he was an owl himself, he saw in his
imagination the birds huddled on branches lower than this one on which he sat. He became
45 an owl himself, he rose and fanned his wings, flew close to the ground, and then swooped,
to rise again with vole or shrew squeaking in his talons. Part-bird then, part-man, he suffered
in the ineluctable predicament of necessary pain and death. The owl could not be blamed;
it lived according to its nature; but its victim must be pitied. This was the terrifying mystery,
why creatures he loved should kill one another. He had been told that all over the world in the
50 war now being fought men, women, and children were being slaughtered in thousands; cities
were being burnt down. He could not understand it, and so he tried, with success, to forget it.

'Well, we'd better make for down,' said Neil at last, with a heavy sigh.

'I could sit up here all night, Neil,' his brother assured him eagerly.

Questions

32. **Using your own words**, summarise the setting described in the extract.
Make at least **four** key points.

4

33. Look again at lines 1–31. Show how any **two** examples of the language of these lines
help to establish the **mood** or **atmosphere** of the novel.

4

34. Look at lines 32–53. How does the language of these lines establish the character of:

(a) Neil?

2

(b) Calum?

2

35. By referring to this extract, and to at least **two** other incidents from elsewhere in the
novel, explain how the theme of nature is explored.

8

SCOTTISH TEXT (POETRY)

If you choose to write on this text in Section A you may not write a critical essay on poetry in Section B.

Read the extract below and then attempt the following questions.

Text 1

War Photographer by Carol Ann Duffy

In his darkroom he is finally alone

with spools of suffering set out in ordered rows.

The only light is red and softly glows,

as though this were a church and he

5   a priest preparing to intone a mass.

Belfast. Beirut. Phnom Penh. All flesh is grass.

He has a job to do. Solutions slop in trays

beneath his hands which did not tremble then

though seem to now. Rural England. Home again

10   to ordinary pain which simple weather can dispel,

to fields which don't explode beneath the feet

of running children in a nightmare heat.

Something is happening. A stranger's features

faintly start to twist before his eyes,

15   a half formed ghost. He remembers the cries

of this man's wife, how he sought approval

without words to do what someone must

and how the blood stained into foreign dust.

A hundred agonies in black-and-white

20   from which his editor will pick out five or six

for Sunday's supplement. The reader's eyeballs prick

with tears between the bath and pre-lunch beers.

From the aeroplane he stares impassively at where

he earns his living and they do not care.

Questions

36. Show how **two** examples of the poet's use of language in lines 1–7 help to establish the main ideas of the poem.

4

37. Show how any **two** examples of the poet's use of language in lines 8–17 effectively contribute to the main ideas or concerns of the poem.

4

38. How effective do you find any aspect of the final six lines as a conclusion to the poem? Your answer might deal with ideas and/or language.

4

39. With close textual reference, show how the ideas and/or language of this poem are similar OR different to another poem or poems by Carol Ann Duffy that you have read.

8

If you choose to write on this text in Section A you may not write a critical essay on poetry in Section B.

Read the extract below and then attempt the following questions.

Text 2

Lucozade **by Jackie Kay**

My mum is on a high bed next to sad chrysanthemums.

'Don't bring flowers, they only wilt and die.'

I am scared my mum is going to die

On the bed next to the sad chrysanthemums.

5   She nods off and her eyes go back in her head.

Next to her bed is a bottle of Lucozade.

'Orange nostalgia, that's what that is,' she says.

'Don't bring Lucozade either,' then fades.

'The whole day was a blur, a swarm of eyes.

10   Those doctors with their white lies.

Did you think you could cheer me up with a *Woman's Own?*

Don't bring magazines, too much about size.'

My mum wakes up, groggy and low.

'What I want to know,' she says, 'is this:

15   Where's the big brandy, the generous gin, the Bloody Mary,

the biscuit tin, the chocolate gingers, the dirty big meringue?'

I am sixteen; I've never tasted a Bloody Mary.

'Tell your father to bring a luxury,' says she.

'Grapes have no imagination, they're just green.

20   Tell him: stop the neighbours coming.'

I clear her cupboard in Ward 10B, Stobhill Hospital.

I leave, bags full, Lucozade, grapes, oranges,

Sad chrysanthemums under my arms,

weighted down. I turn round, wave with her flowers.

25   My mother, on her high hospital bed, waves back.

Her face is light and radiant, dandelion hours.

Her sheets billow and whirl. She is beautiful.

Next to her the empty table is divine.

I carry the orange nostalgia home singing an old song.

Questions

40. Many of the main ideas or concerns of the poem come across clearly in the first three stanzas.

(a)   Identify **two** of these main ideas or concerns from the first three stanzas.   **2**

(b)   Show how **two** examples of the poet's use of language in the first three stanzas help to clarify or illustrate these ideas.   **4**

41. Show how any **two** examples of the poet's use of language in stanza 4 or 5 effectively contributes to the main ideas or concerns of the poem.   **4**

42. How effective do you find any aspect of the final 5 lines as a conclusion to the poem?

Your answer might deal with ideas and/or language.   **2**

43. With close textual reference, show how the ideas and/or language of this poem are similar OR different to another poem or poems by Jackie Kay that you have read.   **8**

If you choose to write on this text in Section A you may not write a critical essay on poetry in Section B.

Read the extract below and then attempt the following questions.

Text 3

Assisi by Norman MacCaig

The dwarf with his hands on backwards

sat, slumped like a half-filled sack

on tiny twisted legs from which

sawdust might run,

5   outside the three tiers of churches built

in honour of St Francis, brother

of the poor, talker with birds, over whom

he had the advantage

of not being dead yet.

10 A priest explained

how clever it was of Giotto

to make his frescoes tell stories

that would reveal to the illiterate the goodness

of God and the suffering

15 of His Son. I understood

the explanation and

the cleverness.

A rush of tourists, clucking contentedly,

fluttered after him as he scattered

20 the grain of the Word. It was they who had passed

the ruined temple outside, whose eyes

wept pus, whose back was higher

than his head, whose lopsided mouth

said *Grazie* in a voice as sweet

25 as a child's when she speaks to her mother

or a bird's when it spoke

to St Francis.

Questions

44. The poem is split into three stanzas, which begin with the words 'The dwarf', 'The priest' and 'A rush of tourists'. **In your own words**, explain clearly what each of these people/ groups of people are doing.

3

45. Show how **two** examples of the poet's use of language in stanza 1 help to clarify or illustrate the main ideas or concerns of the poem.

4

46. How effective do you find the second stanza in developing the main concerns or ideas of the poem?

2

47. What emotional response does the reader feel towards **either** the tourists **or** the beggar? Show how the language of the final stanza creates this response.

3

48. With close textual reference, show how the ideas and/or language of this poem are similar OR different to another poem or poems by Norman MacCaig that you have read.

8

If you choose to write on this text in Section A you may not write a critical essay on poetry in Section B.

Read the extract below and then attempt the following questions.

Text 4

***Trio* by Edwin Morgan**

Coming up Buchanan Street, quickly, on a sharp winter evening

a young man and two girls, under the Christmas lights –

The young man carries a new guitar in his arms,

the girl on the inside carries a very young baby,

5   and the girl on the outside carries a chihuahua.

And the three of them are laughing, their breath rises

in a cloud of happiness, and as they pass

the boy says, 'Wait till he sees this but!'

The chihuahua has a tiny Royal Stewart tartan coat like a teapot-holder,

10   the baby in its white shawl is all bright eyes and mouth like

favours in a fresh sweet cake,

the guitar swells out under its milky plastic cover, tied at the neck

with silver tinsel tape and a brisk sprig of mistletoe.

Orphean sprig! Melting baby! Warm chihuahua!

15   The vale of tears is powerless before you.

Whether Christ is born, or is not born, you

put paid to fate, it abdicates

under the Christmas lights.

Monsters of the year

20   go blank, are scattered back,

can't bear this march of three.

And the three have passed, vanished in the crowd

(yet not vanished, for in their arms they wind

the life of men and beasts, and music,

25   laughter ringing them round like a guard)

at the end of this winter's day.

Questions

49. Many of the main ideas or concerns of the poem come across clearly in the first 13 lines.

   (a) Identify **two** of these main ideas or concerns from these lines.

   2

   (b) Show how **two** examples of the poet's use of language in these lines help to clarify or illustrate his meaning.

   4

50. Show how any **two** examples of the poet's use of language in lines 14–21 effectively contribute to the main ideas or concerns of the poem.

   4

51. How effective do you find any aspect of the final five lines as a conclusion to the poem?

   Your answer might deal with ideas and/or language.

   2

52. With close textual reference, show how the ideas and/or language of this poem are similar OR different to another poem or poems by Edwin Morgan that you have read.

   8

Section B — Critical Essay — 20 marks

Write a critical essay on **one** question from this section of the exam paper. Select your question from **one** of the genres.

You can write on a Scottish text but **not** the same text you answered on in Section A of the exam. You must also write on a different **genre** to the one you selected in Section A.

You have approximately 45 minutes to complete your critical essay.

DRAMA

> *Your answer should refer closely to the text and to important elements such as characterisation, key scene(s), structure, climax, theme, plot, conflict, setting…*

1. Choose a play in which the main character experiences conflict.

    By referring to appropriate techniques, explain what the conflict is, then go on to show how the playwright's portrayal of the conflict influences our response to the play.

2. Choose a play that has an effective opening.

    Describe briefly this opening and then, by referring to appropriate techniques, show how the playwright makes the opening effective.

PROSE

> *Your answer should refer closely to the text and to important elements such as characterisation, setting, language, key incident(s), climax, turning point, plot, structure, narrative technique, theme, ideas, description…*

3. Choose a novel or a short story where an important character clearly shows development or change.

    By referring to appropriate techniques, show how the author has portrayed development and how this influenced your response to the text.

4. Choose a novel or a short story or a work of non-fiction where you can identify a key moment, such as a turning point or climax.

    By referring to appropriate techniques, describe the key moment and then go on to discuss its importance to the text as a whole.

POETRY

Answers to questions in this part should refer to the text and to such relevant features as word choice, tone, imagery, structure, content, rhythm, rhyme, theme, sound, ideas…

5. Choose a poem which describes a character or person who creates an emotional response in the reader.

   Explain briefly who this person is and then describe how the use of poetic techniques influences your response to this person.

6. Choose a poem in which setting is a significant feature.

   Explain briefly what this setting is and then go on to describe the importance of the setting to the poem's central concerns.

FILM and TV DRAMA*

Your answer should refer closely to the text and to important features such as use of camera, key sequence, characterisation, mise-en-scène, editing, setting, music/sound, special effects, plot, dialogue…

7. Choose a film or TV drama that has an interesting central character.

   By referring to appropriate techniques, explain how the film or television makers portray this character.

8. Choose a film or TV drama that uses the conventions of a specific genre such as horror, science fiction, western, etc.

   By referring to appropriate techniques, explain how the conventions are used and/or subverted.

* 'TV drama' includes a single play, a series or a serial.

LANGUAGE STUDY

Your answer should refer closely to the text and to important features such as register, accent, dialect, slang, jargon, vocabulary, tone, abbreviation…

9. Choose a variety of English used in a particular geographical area.

   By referring to specific examples, show how the language differs from Standard English and what advantages and/or disadvantages this offers for its speakers.

10. Consider **two** texts that deal with the same subject matter in contrasting ways, for example two different newspapers, websites, TV programmes.

By referring to specific examples from your chosen texts, show how the way the texts use language is different and discuss the effect of these differences on their intended audience.

[END OF QUESTION PAPER]

Practice Exam C

ENGLISH

NATIONAL 5

Exam C

Reading for Understanding, Analysis and Evaluation

Date — Not applicable

Duration — 1 hour

Total marks: 30

Read the extract and then answer the questions in your own words as much as possible. Try to answer all of the questions.

Square roots

The following article by Ross Martin, which was published in the Sunday Herald, is about the importance of city squares to cities around the world and in Scotland.

We are who we were.

Genetically, culturally, socially, our character is conditioned by our parents, grandparents and more distant family.

We are rooted in the wider community which shaped them and also, crucially, in the place in
5   which they lived. People and place are connected umbilically; we are influenced by the place in which we live as much as we shape our environment.

In the TV series *Who Do You Think You Are?* this link between people and place is analysed, albeit through the looking glass of celebrity, untangling the double helix which is our defining DNA and providing tantalising glimpses into the long-gone towns and villages where our ancestors
10   lived and died.

This connection between people and place is felt keenly in our hearts every time we return home after being away. That warm attachment to home never wavers. In fact, our relationships with each other are conditioned by our relationships with the places in which we live.

They help to make us who we are, so our personalities draw upon any historical connection,
15   and we suffer from a deficit where none exists. This symbiotic relationship describes, nurtures and develops our character as individuals and as a people. It also determines the character and identity of the villages, towns and cities in which we live.

Why is it then that Scotland, alone in a world peppered with wonderful city squares, just can't seem to get these places right? What is it about the politics of our cities that means we have failed
20   miserably to design these civic spaces as places which reflect the character of our communities?

At their best, public squares are the beating heart of the city: a magnet for overseas visitors, a place where local people gather informally from day to day, or at those critical, historic times which define a city, or even a country.

From Tahrir in Cairo to Tiananmen in Beijing, and even London's Trafalgar, the great city squares
25   are places towards which people naturally gravitate when they need to express their collective will, to demonstrate, to demand. City squares are the focal points for democracy, often the place in which it is born. They symbolise society, providing a platform for expression.

In Venice's Piazza San Marco (St Mark's), a classic mix of cultural activity tells the story of this city and its people. From the Doge's Palace on its east flank to the open-air cafe which lights up the
30   southern side with chamber music at lunchtime, St Mark's lives and breathes the life of Venice. All around, arteries course outwards, carrying the visitor through the streets and along the canals of this mesmerising place.

The square has, literally, a central place in the life of Venice. It is the focal point for the millions of tourists who come to taste the culture, to spend time soaking up the atmosphere, and perhaps
35   carry away a little treasure. Whether it's a glistening piece of hand-crafted locally blown Murano glass or a black-and-white striped figurine to remind them of a trip on a gondola, these cultural

connectors are all available in or around the square. St Mark's is also a place where people gather for concerts, theatre and, of course, for the magnificent masked ball.

40 Then there is Times Square in New York: bright, bold, perhaps even brash, it announces loudly and proudly to the world that this is the city that never sleeps. The flashing neon lights, the blaring horns of yellow cabs and the general buzz create an atmosphere which accurately describes the character of this great city. Appropriately, the square is an advert for The Big Apple, a bite-sized taster of the city.

45 Times Square is much more than a convenient through-route. It is a place where people want to linger, meet and chat. It tells us as much about New York as the Empire State Building or the Statue of Liberty. Like Moscow's Red Square, Amsterdam's Dam Square and many other great city squares, it connects with its people, and plays a prominent role in their lives.

In Scotland, such places tend to be one-dimensional. Many of our cities don't even have public squares, and those that exist often give the appearance of just happening to be there, rather than
50 having been designed as the social, cultural and political heart of the metropolis.

Why, then, have we failed so dismally to design the bold and beautiful civic spaces that characterise the world's greatest cities? As other cities continue to nurture, renew and regenerate their great civic spaces, or even create splendid new ones, Scotland once again stumbles, staggers and slumps into another embarrassing demonstration of how not to do it. George
55 Square, currently dominated by traffic, is a crossing point rather than a gathering place. In the evenings, it doesn't function as other city squares do. As the neighbouring Queen Street railway station prepares for a right royal makeover, which will hopefully see the demolition of those concrete carbuncles on its square face, what an opportunity to reclaim the streets around it for people. Create a place where people can linger comfortably and safely, meet and greet, eat and
60 relax, ponder and chill. Make the square fit for its rightful role as a modern, vibrant centre-point for cultural, social and economic interactions.

City squares the world over are the beating hearts of their communities. They are the places where people gather in times of celebration and at points of crisis too. Who can forget the displays of Soviet military might goose-stepping through Red Square? Remember the iconic
65 image of the lone, flag-waving protester facing down the tanks of the Chinese Army in Tiananmen Square? More recently, Cairo's Tahrir Square, as the focal point of the 2011 Egyptian Revolution, has helped define the early days of democracy in that troubled place.

City squares are where history is made. They shape who we are, but they must also reflect who we want to be. Why is it that Scotland can't get four-square behind these symbols of civic pride?
70 Certainly elected mayors may help, but until we join the rest of the civilised world in that area, we need a different way to reconnect people and place. Anyone for a square go?

Civic squares are a defining characteristic of the world's great cities. Why can't Scotland get them right?

Adapted from an article by Ross Martin in the Sunday Herald, Sunday 10 February 2013.

Questions

1. (a) 'We are who we were' (line 1). **In your own words**, explain how the writer expands on this idea in lines 2–17.

    2

    (b) Explain how the writer's word choice in these lines helps to convey these ideas.

    4

2. What is the difference between city squares in the rest of the world and in Scotland according to lines 18–20? **Use your own words** as far as possible.

    2

3. Look at lines 21–23. **In your own words**, say what the writer believes the purpose of city squares to be.

    2

4. Referring to lines 28–47, describe, **using your own words**, what the writer admires about St Mark's in Venice and Times Square in New York.

    4

5. Referring to **two** examples, explain how the writer uses word choice to evoke the excitement of Times Square.

    4

6. Look at lines 51–61. Identify the writer's attitude to George Square and show how the writer's use of language expresses this attitude.

    2

7. Look at lines 51–61. **In your own words**, explain clearly what the writer believes would improve George Square.

    3

8. Choose **one** of the following images:

    'untangling the double helix which is our defining DNA'

    Times Square is 'a bite-sized taster of the city'

    'Scotland once again stumbles, staggers and slumps'

    Explain what your chosen image means and analyse its effect.

    3

9. Referring to the whole article, **in your own words** list the key points the writer makes about city squares around the world and George Square in particular.

    4

[END OF QUESTION PAPER]

Practice Papers for SQA Exams

ENGLISH
NATIONAL 5
Exam C
Critical Reading

Date — Not applicable

Duration — 1 hour and 30 minutes

Total marks: 40

Section A: Scottish Text – 20 marks

Choose an extract from a Scottish text you have studied and then answer the questions. Try to complete all of the questions.

Choose only **one** text from either Part A Drama, Part B Prose or Part C Poetry.

Section B: Critical Essay – 20 marks

Write **one** critical essay on a text you have studied from one of the genres of Drama, Prose, Poetry, Film and TV Drama or Language Study.

You are permitted to write an essay on a text from the list of Scottish texts, providing that you have not written about the same text in Section A and that the genre you select is not the same as the one you answered on in Section A.

Each section of the exam should take approximately 45 minutes to complete.

Section A — Scottish Text — 20 marks

Answer the questions from **one** of the three sections only (Drama, Prose or Poetry).

Read the text carefully and then answer **all** of the questions on the text, writing the answers in your own words as much as possible.

SCOTTISH TEXT (DRAMA)

If you choose to write on this text in Section A you may not write a critical essay on drama in Section B.

Read the extract below and then attempt the following questions.

Text 1

Bold Girls by Rona Munro

	CASSIE:	How do you stand it here Marie?
	MARIE:	Sure where else would I go?
	CASSIE:	How do you keep that smile on your face?
	MARIE:	Super-glue.
5	CASSIE:	There's not one bit of bitterness in you, is there?
	MARIE:	Oh Cassie.
	CASSIE:	You see, you're good. And I'm just wicked.
	MARIE:	Aye you're a bold woman altogether.
	CASSIE:	Is it hard being good?
10	MARIE:	I took lessons.
	CASSIE:	Well, tell me what you've got to smile about Marie, because I'm sure I can't see it.
	MARIE:	I've a lot to be thankful for. I've my kids, a job, a nice wee house and I can still pay for it.
15	CASSIE:	You've two wee boys growing out of their clothes faster than you can get them new ones, a part-time job licking envelopes for a wage that couldn't keep a budgie and three red bills on your mantelpiece there.
	MARIE:	That's what's great about a Saturday night out with you Cassie, you just know how to look at the bright side of things, don't you?
20	CASSIE:	Well just tell me how you can keep filling that kettle and making folk tea without pouring it over their head?
	MARIE:	Ah well you see, I'm a mug.
	CASSIE:	I think you are.
	MARIE:	I didn't marry Joe, but…

	CASSIE:	No. You did not. That mug was me.
25	MARIE:	See Cassie, I've had better times with Michael than a lot of women get in their whole lives with a man.
	CASSIE:	And that keeps you going?
	MARIE:	It's a warming kind of thought.

Cassie holds out her arms to Michael's pictures.

30	CASSIE:	*(singing)* Thanks for the memories.
	MARIE:	Oh Cassie.
	CASSIE:	That doesn't work, Marie. I've tried to keep myself warm that way. Find some man with good hands and warm skin and wrap him round you to keep the rain off; you'll be damp in the end anyway.
35	MARIE:	Cassie, don't talk like that; you know you've not done half the wild things you make out.
	CASSIE:	Not a quarter of what I've wanted to Marie, but enough to know it doesn't work. Grabbing onto some man because he smells like excitement, he smells like escape. They can't take you anywhere except into the back seat of their car. They're all
40		the same.
	MARIE:	If that's what you think of them that'll be all you'll find.

Cassie gets up to stand, looking at Michael.

	CASSIE:	They are *all* the same, Marie.

Questions

1. **In your own words**, summarise:

   (a) Marie's reasons for staying where she is.

   2

   (b) Cassie's criticisms of Marie's life.

   2

2. With close reference to the text, explain how the playwright reveals the character of:

   (a) Marie

   2

   (b) Cassie

   4

3. Marie and Cassie have been best friends for years. However, in this extract there is conflict between them.
   With close reference to the text, explain how the playwright reveals this conflict.

   2

4. By referring to this extract, and to at least **two** other incidents from elsewhere in the play, explain how the character of Cassie develops as the story progresses and her significance to the play as a whole.

   8

If you choose to write on this text in Section A you may not write a critical essay on drama in Section B.

Read the extract below and then attempt the following questions.

Text 2

***Tally's Blood* by Ann Marie di Mambro**

Pick up on ginger store: Hughie deeply engrossed in tidying crates. Stops and surveys it with satisfaction. Takes a bottle of ginger and drinks from it. Enter Lucia, indignant when she sees him. She goes right up to him, eyeing him up and down suspiciously: Hughie keeps drinking from the bottle.

5

LUCIA: (*Increasingly self-righteous*) Hughie Devlin! What are you doing here?… Who says you could come in here?… This is my Uncle Massimo's ginger store… This is my Uncle Massimo's whole shop, so it is… Everything in here is my Uncle Massimo's… Did you ask for that ginger?…That's my Uncle Massimo's ginger… I'm going to tell my Uncle Massimo on you… I'm telling him you took his ginger… You better not take any more of that ginger…

10   *Hughie takes the bottle from his mouth and involuntarily lets out an almighty belch: she is horrified, punches him on the upper arm.*

LUCIA: You stop that you!

Hughie hands her the bottle.

HUGHIE: Want a slug?

15   *Lucia turns away in disgust.*

LUCIA: No thank you.

HUGHIE: You can if you want. It's my ginger.

Lucia scoffs.

HUGHIE: Honest. It is. Mr Pedreschi says I'd to help myself.

20   LUCIA: How come?

HUGHIE: (*Chuffed*) Because I work here that's how come.

LUCIA: You do not.

HUGHIE: I do so. (*A beat*) Want a slug?

25   *Lucia eyes the bottle then slowly takes it: she makes a great show of wiping the top of it with the palm of her hand. Looks Hughie in the eye then does it again, very hard. Then she pulls the sleeve of her jumper down over her hand and rubs the bottle feverishly with it before deigning to put it to her lips. She takes a dainty little sip. Hughie watches carefully. She takes another little sip. Finally she tilts her*

head back and takes huge gulps, thoroughly enjoying it. Hughie is right up to her, examining the bottle and her progress with its contents with some concern.

30 HUGHIE: If you get my chewing gum in your mouth will you spit it back into the bottle?

With a horrified scream, Lucia stops, spits out the liquid from her mouth, showering Hughie.

Questions

5. Hughie has just been given a job in Massimo's shop.

    With close reference to the text, explain how the playwright reveals Hughie's feelings towards his work.

    4

6. Look at lines 1–9. With close reference to the text, explain how the playwright reveals Lucia's reaction to discovering Hughie in the ginger store.

    4

7. Look at the stage directions, '*Lucia eyes the bottle… some concern.*'

    In your own words, explain how Lucia's treatment of the bottle of ginger changes.

    2

8. Look at lines 30–31. With close reference to the text, show how the writer creates comedy in these lines.

    2

9. By referring to this extract, and to at least **two** other incidents from elsewhere in the play, explain how the relationship between Lucia and Hughie develops.

    8

If you choose to write on this text in Section A you may not write a critical essay on drama in Section B.

Read the extract below and then attempt the following questions.

Text 3

Sailmaker **by Alan Spence**

This extract comes from the first act. Ian and Alec have been playing football.

	IAN:	Imagine *really* being a fitba player. Getting *paid* for it! Be better than anything.
	ALEC:	Best job in the whole world.
	IAN:	Better than being a painter!
	ALEC:	Or a sailmaker.
5	IAN:	Or a tick man.

(They exit, DAVIE and BILLY enter, opposite sides of stage)

	BILLY:	What's up wi your face?

(DAVIE shakes head)

		What's the matter?
10	DAVIE:	Ah just got ma jotters. Week's notice.
	BILLY:	Jesus Christ! What for?
	DAVIE:	Ach! They're saying the book's a dead loss. They're gonnae shut it awthegither. Put the sherriff's officers on tae folk that still owe money.
	BILLY:	Bastards.
15	DAVIE:	Gettin that doin just finished it. Losin the money an the ledgers an everythin.
	BILLY:	But that wasnae your fault!
	DAVIE:	Try tellin them that! So that's me. Scrubbed. Again. Laid off. Redundant. Services no longer required. Just like that. Ah don't know. Work aw yer days an what've ye got tae show for it? Turn roon an kick ye in the teeth. Ah mean, what have ye got when ye come right down tae it. Nothin.
20		
	BILLY:	Ah might be able tae get ye a start in our place. Cannae promise mind ye. An if there was anything it wouldnae be much. Maybe doin yer sweeper up or that.
	DAVIE:	Anythin's better than nothing.
	BILLY:	An once yer in the place, ye never know. Somethin better might come up.
25	DAVIE:	*(Dead)* Aye.
	BILLY:	Likes ae a storeman's job or that.
	DAVIE:	Aye.

BILLY: We never died a winter yet, eh?

(*DAVIE nods. BILLY exits*)

30 DAVIE: Scrubbed. Get yer jacket on. Pick up yer cards. On yer way pal! Out the door.

(*ALEC is playing with a yacht, positions fid like bowsprit, bow like mast, tries to make 'sail' with cellophane, can't hold all the separate bits, drops them. DAVIE comes in behind him*)

Bit of bad news son.

35 (*Pause*)

Ah've lost ma job. They gave me ma books.

DAVIE: Billy says he might be able tae fix me up wi somethin. Wouldnae be much. (*Shrugs*) Better than nothing. Ach that was a lousy job anyway. Ah'm better off out ae it. Whatever happens.

40 Place is a right mess eh. Amazin how it gets on top of ye.

ALEC: Ah'll shove this in the glory hole. Out the road.

(*Folds up cellophane, puts tools in bag and picks up bow, yacht, carries the lot and exits*)

DAVIE: Ach aye. Not to worry. Never died a winter yet.

45 (*Fade lights. Two notes on mouth organ, fade*)

Questions

10. Look at lines 1–5. At this stage in the play Ian and Alec are still young and optimistic. How does the language of these lines convey this?

2

11. Look at lines 7–30. Davie has just been made redundant from his job. Show how the writer's language conveys the reactions of:

(a) Davie

4

(b) Billy

4

12. Look at lines 34–43. Explain clearly how Davie gives a different reaction when speaking to Alec.

2

13. At the beginning of this extract Ian and Alec are playing together. With close reference to the rest of the play, explain how the relationship between Ian and Alec develops.

8

SCOTTISH TEXT (PROSE)

If you choose to write on this text in Section A you may not write a critical essay on prose in Section B.

Read the extract below and then attempt the following questions.

Text 1

The Painter by Iain Crichton Smith

At the beginning of this extract, tensions between Red Roderick and his father-in-law finally explode into violence.

After he had paced about outside his house for a while shouting and throwing things, he seemed to make up his mind and went down to the byre from which he emerged with a scythe. At first I thought – since I was his neighbour – that he was going to scythe the corn but this was not at all what was in his mind. No, he set off with the scythe in his hand as if it was made of glass. When
5 he got to the house he shouted out to the old man that it was time he came out and fought like a man, if he was as great as people said he had been in the past. There was, apart from his voice, a great silence all over the village which drowsed in the sun as he made his challenge. The day in fact was so calm that there was an atmosphere as if one was in church, and it seemed that he was disturbing it in exactly the same way as a shouting lunatic might do who entered a church during
10 a service.

One or two people said that someone should go for a policeman but no one in fact did. In any case looking back on it now I think that in a strange shameful way we were looking forward to the result of the challenge as if it would be a break in an endless routine. Nevertheless there was something really frightening and irresponsible about Red Roderick that day as if all the poison
15 that seethed around his system had emerged to the surface as cloudy dregs will float upwards to the surface of bad liquor. Strangely enough – in response to the shouting, as in a Western – the old man did come out and he too shared in the madness which was shattering the silence of the day. Then they began to fight.

As Red Roderick was drunk perhaps the advantage given by relative youth was to a certain
20 extent cancelled. There was however no doubt that he wished to kill the old man, so enraged was he, so frustrated by the life that tortured him. As they swung their scythes towards each other ponderously, it looked at first as if they could do little harm, and indeed it was odd to see them, as if each was trying to cut corn. However, after some time – while the face of the old man gradually grew more demoniac in a renewal of his youth – he succeeded at last in cutting his son-in-law's
25 left leg so that he fell to the ground, his wife running towards him like an old hen, her skirts trailing the ground like broken wings.

But that was not what I meant to tell since the fight in itself, though unpleasant, was not evil. No, as I stood in the ring with the others, excited and horrified, I saw on the edge of the ring young William with his paint-brush and canvas and easel painting the fight. He was sitting comfortably
30 on a chair which he had taken with him and there was no expression on his face at all but a cold clear intensity which bothered me. It seemed in a strange way as if we were asleep. As the scythes swung to and fro, as the faces of the antagonists became more and more contorted in the fury of

battle, as their cheeks were suffused with blood and rage, and their teeth were drawn back in a snarl, he sat there painting the battle, nor any time did he make any attempt to pull his chair back
35 from the arena where they were engaged.

I cannot explain to you the feelings that seethed through me as I watched him. One feeling was partly admiration that he should be able to concentrate with such intensity that he didn't seem able to notice the danger he was in. The other feeling was one of the most bitter disgust as if I were watching a gaze that had gone beyond the human and which was as indifferent to
40 the outcome as a hawk's might be. You may think I was wrong in what I did next. I deliberately came up behind him and upset the chair so that he fell down head over heels in the middle of a brush-stroke. He turned on me such a gaze of blind fury that I was reminded of a rat which had once leaped at me from a river bank, and he would have struck me but that I pinioned his arms behind his back. I would have beaten him if his mother hadn't come and taken him away,
45 still snarling and weeping tears of rage. In spite of my almost religious fear at that moment, I tore the painting into small pieces and scattered them about the earth. Some people have since said that what I wanted to do was to protect the good name of the village but I must in all honesty say that that was not in my mind when I pushed the chair over. All that was in my mind was fury and disgust that this painter should have watched this fight with such cold
50 concentration that he seemed to think that the fight had been set up for him to paint, much as a house exists or an old wall.

Questions

14. **In your own words**, explain why the narrator is mistaken about what Red Roderick plans to do with the scythe.

2

15. Look at lines 1–18. Show how any **two** examples of the writer's use of language effectively convey the emotions of Red Roderick.

4

16. Look at lines 27–35. How does the writer convey that the painter's reaction is different to the other spectators?

2

17. Show how **two** examples of the writer's word choice effectively convey the aggression of the narrator.

4

18. With close textual reference, show how the ideas and/or language of this short story are similar OR different to another story or stories by Iain Crichton Smith that you have read.

8

If you choose to write on this text in Section A you may not write a critical essay on prose in Section B.

Read the extract below and then attempt the following questions.

Text 2

A Chitterin Bite **by Anne Donovan**

We go tae the pictures every week efter the swimmin, scramblin tae get the chummy seats up the back, sharing wer sweeties, grabbing each other's airms at the scary bits and gigglin at the love scenes. Then wan week, when we're walkin alang the road efter the baths, Agnes says:

Ah said we'd meet Jimmy McKeown and his pal at the pictures.

5   *What?*

He wants tae go wi me. He says he'll bring his pal for you.

Do you want tae go wi him?

Ah don't know, ah'll gie it a try.

Ah unlinked ma airm fae Agnes's and marched on, starin ahead.

10   *Well, you don't need me tae come too.*

Agnes caught up wi me, grabbing at ma airm.

Ah cannae go masel.

How no?

Ah just cannae. Anyway, he's bringin his pal. If you don't go, ah cannae go. Come on, Mary, be a pal.

15   The boys are waitin for us inside the foyer of the picture hoose. Jimmy McKeown is a year aulder than us, wi a broad nose, a bit bent tae the side, and straight dirty-fair hair in a side shed. The pal is staunin hauf behind him, a wee skinny laddie wi roond baby cheeks and red lips like a lassie.

This is Shuggie, he's ma cousin.

This is Mary.

20   *Hiya.*

Will we go in?

After yous, girls.

They're polite, even though Jimmy is actin the big shot and the pal still hasnae opened his mooth. Agnes leadin the way tae the back row where the chummy seats are. She sits doon in wan but
25   when ah go tae sit next tae her she mutters *naw, you huvtae sit wi Shuggie* and shoves me ower tae the next seat, where the airm rest forms a barrier between me and her. Ah feel Shuggie's knees pushin intae mines as he squeezes by me tae sit in the other hauf of the seat. Ah move as

far ower tae the side nearest Agnes as ah can, but ah cannae help smellin the rough hairy smell of his sports jacket under the sourness of the aftershave he must of plastered on his baby cheeks.

30   I don't expect the phone call. Not so soon anyway, not at work, not at ten o'clock in the morning, sitting at my bright shiny desk with my red folder in front of me and my bright, shiny perfectly modulated work voice:

Good morning, Mary Henderson speaking, how may I help you?

Mary? It's me, Matthew, listen, I've got to talk to you, it's urgent. Can you meet me for lunch?

35   *Of course.*

Look, I can't talk now. Can you meet me in Sarti's? One o'clock?

OK. Make it quarter to, though, you know how busy it gets there.

Right. See you then.

*

40   At lunchtime Sarti's is full of people in suits from nearby offices and the atmosphere is warm and faintly smoky. We sit down at a table just opposite the deli counter, which is piled high with different kinds of *panettone*. Matthew looks immaculate in his grey suit and silk floral tie but, as he bends his head to look at the menu, I notice a few stray bristly hairs, just where his cheekbone joins his neck, which he must have missed when shaving this morning. He looks at the menu as he speaks.

45   *What are you having?*

Spaghetti vongole, I think. I'm starving. Maybe a night of passion makes you hungry.

He looks up but does not smile.

I don't have time for lunch. I think I'll just have coffee and a bit of cake.

A chitterin bite.

50   *What?*

It's what we used to call a bite to eat, not a full meal, just enough to keep the cold out after the swimming.

He folds the menu up and replaces it in its holder.

Speaking of bites…

55   I look him straight in the eyes.

Mary, do you know what kind of mark you left on me last night?

Did I?

He squeezes his left hand tight into a fist, then releases it, repeating the movement several times as though it were an exercise.

Questions

19. Look at lines 1–29.

    (a) What happens in this extract from the novel? Make at least **two** key points.

        2

    (b) Show how **two** examples of the writer's use of language effectively convey Mary's changing emotions in these lines.

        4

20. Look at lines 30–59.

    (a) What happens in these lines from the novel? Make at least **two** key points.

        2

    (b) Show how the writer's use of language effectively conveys Mary's changing emotions in these lines.

        2

    (c) Explain how the writer uses language to create a sense of suspense in these lines.

        2

21. By referring to this extract and the story *A Chitterin Bite* as a whole, explain how the ideas/language are similar OR different to at least **one** other story by Anne Donovan you have read.

        8

If you choose to write on this text in Section A you may not write a critical essay on prose in Section B.

Read the extract below and then attempt the following questions.

Text 3

The Testament of Gideon Mack **by James Robertson**

In this extract, Gideon and his friend John are returning from the hospital where Gideon has just identified the body of his wife, Jenny, who has died in a car crash.

We hardly spoke all the way back to Monimaskit. John drove with infinite care, as if somehow that would help. I thought, someone is killed in one of these things, and the first thing we do is get in another one and drive to see the body, then drive away again. We have no option: our lives depend on machines that kill us. And I remembered an image from the news item about
5   Ravenscraig, a rush of molten steel coming at the camera.

'She looked very beautiful, Gideon,' John said. 'She looked like she was at peace.'

'Aye, John, aye. Fine words. She looks like that because she's dead.'

After a minute I said, 'I'm sorry, that was uncalled for. You're right. I hope you're right.'

There are two routes between Monimaskit and Dundee, both about the same distance. We had
10   gone one way, and drove back the other. We were halfway through the Glack, with its wooded slopes running steeply down the road on either side, before I realised where we were. It was very dark. 'It was here somewhere,' I said. 'Can you see anything?' John slowed down, and on a short bit of straight before one of the sharpest bends he came almost to a complete halt. Had it been here? From what the police had said I thought so. We stared, but there was no evidence. The wreckage
15   had been cleared away and the road in the headlights' glare looked as it always had done. Nothing was different. Everything had changed. I heard my mother say, 'This life isn't about happiness. It simply isn't important.' My father's voice thudded against the inside of my forehead, his phrase about confronting one's own immortality. I stared into the darkness. Jenny's body was lying in Ninewells Hospital, but was a part of her wandering out there somewhere? I felt like getting out,
20   going to look for her, but John picked up speed again and I said nothing.

Elsie met us at the manse, red-eyed. She hugged me, then I got out the house-keys and gave them to her and we went in. The house was more than just empty; it was as if no one had lived there for years. Elsie wanted to collect some clothes, a toothbrush. 'You're coming back with us,' she said. 'You're not staying here tonight.'

25   'I've got things to do,' I said. 'It's half-past ten. It's too late and there's nothing they can do. Let them sleep.'

The light on the answer machine in the study was flashing. I moved towards it.

'Get in the car,' Elsie said. 'There's nothing there that can't wait.'

John and I went out, and Elsie followed a minute later, switching off the lights and locking the
30   door behind her. John had the engine running. 'Let's go,' Elsie said. The wheels spun on the gravel.

You'd have thought we were in a gangster movie, that we had a plan, except that when Elsie got in the back with me and took my hand and squeezed it hard we both started crying as if we were children lost in the forest in the middle of a horrible fairy tale.

Questions

22. Summarise the different ways Gideon reacts to his grief in this extract from the novel. Make at least **three** key points.

3

23. Look at lines 1–8. What is the mood or atmosphere between Gideon and John at this point in the novel, and how does the writer use language effectively to create this mood or atmosphere?

3

24. Look at lines 9–20. Gideon tries to keep his emotions under control here. Show how the writer effectively conveys Gideon's suppressed emotions.

4

25. Look at lines 21–33. How does the writer use language effectively to convey the way Gideon's emotions change during this section?

2

26. By referring to this extract, and to at least **two** other incidents from elsewhere in the novel, explain how the writer depicts Gideon's relationships with women and their significance to the novel as a whole.

8

If you choose to write on this text in Section A you may not write a critical essay on prose in Section B.

Read the extract below and then attempt the following questions.

Text 4

Kidnapped by Robert Louis Stevenson

In this extract the narrator, David Balfour, finds the house of Shaws, where he believes he will receive his inheritance.

I sat me down and stared at the house of Shaws. The more I looked, the pleasanter that country-side appeared; being all set with hawthorn bushes full of flowers; the fields dotted with sheep; a fine flight of rooks in the sky; and every sign of a kind soil and climate; and yet the barrack in the midst of it went sore against my fancy.

5   Country folk went by from the fields as I sat there on the side of the ditch, but I lacked the spirit to give them a good-e'en. At last the sun went down, and then, right up against the yellow sky, I saw a scroll of smoke go mounting, not much thicker, as it seemed to me, than the smoke of a candle; but still there it was, and meant a fire, and warmth, and cookery, and some living inhabitant that must have lit it; and this comforted my heart.

10   So I set forward by a little faint track in the grass that led in my direction. It was very faint indeed to be the only way to a place of habitation; yet I saw no other. Presently it brought me to stone uprights, with an unroofed lodge beside them, and coats of arms upon the top. A main entrance it was plainly meant to be, but never finished; instead of gates of wrought iron, a pair of hurdles were tied across with a straw rope; and as there were no park walls, nor any sign of avenue, the track that
15   I was following passed on the right hand of the pillars, and went wandering on toward the house.

The nearer I got to that, the drearier it appeared. It seemed like the one wing of a house that had never been finished. What should have been the inner end stood open on the upper floors, and showed against the sky with steps and stairs of uncompleted masonry. Many of the windows were unglazed, and bats flew in and out like doves out of a dove-cote.

20   The night had begun to fall as I got close; and in three of the lower windows, which were very high up and narrow, and well barred, the changing light of a little fire began to glimmer. Was this the palace I had been coming to? Was it within these walls that I was to seek new friends and begin great fortunes? Why, in my father's house on Essen-Waterside, the fire and the bright lights would show a mile away, and the door open to a beggar's knock!

25   I came forward cautiously, and giving ear as I came, heard someone rattling with dishes, and a little dry, eager cough that came in fits; but there was no sound of speech, and not a dog barked.

The door, as well as I could see it in the dim light, was a great piece of wood all studded with nails; and I lifted my hand with a faint heart under my jacket, and knocked once. Then I stood and waited. The house had fallen into a dead silence; a whole minute passed away, and nothing stirred
30   but the bats overhead. I knocked again, and hearkened again. By this time my ears had grown so accustomed to the quiet, that I could hear the ticking of the clock inside as it slowly counted out the seconds; but whoever was in that house kept deadly still, and must have held his breath.

I was in two minds whether to run away; but anger got the upper hand, and I began instead to rain kicks and buffets on the door, and to shout out aloud for Mr Balfour. I was in full career, when
35   I heard the cough right overhead, and jumping back and looking up, beheld a man's head in a tall nightcap, and the bell mouth of a blunderbuss, at one of the first-storey windows.

'It's loaded,' said a voice.

'I have come here with a letter,' I said, 'to Mr Ebenezer Balfour of Shaws. Is he here?'

'From whom is it?' asked the man with the blunderbuss.

40   'That is neither here nor there,' said I, for I was growing very wroth.

'Well,' was the reply, 'ye can put it down upon the doorstep, and be off with ye.'

'I will do no such thing,' I cried. 'I will deliver it into Mr Balfour's hands, as it was meant I should. It is a letter of introduction.'

'A what?' cried the voice, sharply.

45   I repeated what I had said.

'Who are ye, yourself?' was the next question, after a considerable pause.

'I am not ashamed of my name,' said I. 'They call me David Balfour.'

At that, I made sure the man started, for I heard the blunderbuss rattle on the window-sill; and it was after quite a long pause, and with a curious change of voice, that the next question followed:

50   'Is your father dead?'

I was so much surprised at this, that I could find no voice to answer, but stood staring.

'Ay' the man resumed, 'he'll be dead, no doubt; and that'll be what brings ye chapping to my door.' Another pause, and then defiantly, 'Well, man,' he said, 'I'll let ye in,' and he disappeared from the window.

Questions

27. Summarise what happens in this extract from the novel. Make at least **three** key points.

3

28. Look at the first paragraph. How does the writer's language show the contrast between the house of Shaws and its surroundings?

4

29. Look at lines 17–32. What is the mood or atmosphere created by the writer, and how does the writer use language effectively to create this mood or atmosphere?

3

30. Look at lines 37–54. How is the character of Ebenezer revealed through word choice?

2

31. By referring to this extract, and to at least **two** other incidents from elsewhere in the novel, explain how the character of David changes and develops as the story progresses.

8

If you choose to write on this text in Section A you may not write a critical essay on prose in Section B.

Read the extract below and then attempt the following questions.

Text 5

The Cone-Gatherers **by Robin Jenkins**

In this extract Neil and Calum are sheltering from a storm in the beach hut, which belongs to Lady Runcie-Campbell.

Neil went over to attend to the fire.

'Get your jacket off, Calum,' he said, 'and hold it in front of the fire.'

As he spoke he was cautiously taking his own off. His shoulder joints were very stiff and sore.

'Do you know what I'm going to do?' he asked, as he was helping to take off his brother's jacket. 5 'I'm going to have a puff at that pipe you bought me in Lendrick.'

Calum was delighted. 'Is it a good pipe, Neil?'

'The best I ever had. It must have cost you a fortune.'

Calum laughed and shook his head. 'I'm not telling,' he said.

Neil was feeling in his pocket for the pipe when other noises outside were added to the 10 drumming of the rain on the roof: a dog's bark, and voices.

As they stared towards the door, there came a scratching on it as of paws, and a whining. A minute later they heard the lady cry out: 'Thank God!' and then a key rattled in the lock. The door was flung open to the accompaniment of the loudest peal of thunder since the start of the storm.

From a safe distance the little dog barked at the trespassers. The lady had only a silken 15 handkerchief over her head; her green tweed costume was black in places with damp. In the midst of the thunder she shouted: 'What is the meaning of this?' Though astonishment, and perhaps dampness, made her voice hoarse, it nevertheless was far more appalling to the two men than any thunder. They could not meet the anger in her face. They gazed at her feet; her stockings were splashed with mud and her shoes had sand on them.

20 Neil did not know what to do or say. Every second of silent abjectness was a betrayal of himself, and especially of his brother who was innocent. All his vows of never again being ashamed of Calum were being broken. His rheumatism tortured him, as if coals from the stolen fire had been pressed into his shoulders and knees; but he wished that the pain was twenty times greater to punish him as he deserved. He could not lift his head; he tried, so that he could meet the lady's 25 gaze at least once, no matter how scornful and contemptuous it was; but he could not. A lifetime of frightened submissiveness held it down.

Suddenly he realised that Calum was speaking.

'It's not Neil's fault, lady,' he was saying. 'He did it because I was cold and wet.'

'For God's sake,' muttered the lady, and Neil felt rather than saw how she recoiled from Calum, as if
30 from something obnoxious, and took her children with her. For both the boy and girl were present.

The dog had not stopped barking.

Even that insult to Calum could not break the grip shame had of Neil. Still with lowered head, he
dragged on his jacket.

'Get out,' cried the lady. 'For God's sake, get out.'

35 Neil had to help Calum on with his jacket. Like an infant Calum presented the wrong hand, so that
they had to try again. The girl giggled but the boy said nothing.

At last they were ready.

'I'll have to get my cones,' whispered Calum.

'Get them.'

40 Calum went over and picked up the bag lying beside the hamper of toys.

Neil led the way past the lady, who drew back. He mumbled he was sorry.

Calum repeated the apology.

She stood in the doorway and gazed out at them running away into the rain. The dog barked
after them from the edge of the veranda.

45 'You'll hear more about this,' she said.

In the hut Sheila had run to the fire, with little groans of joy. From the corner to which he had
retreated Roderick watched her, with his own face grave and tense.

Their mother came in and shut the door.

'I shall certainly see to it,' she said, 'that they don't stay long in the wood after this. This week will
50 be their last, whatever Mr Tulloch may say. I never heard of such impertinence.' She had to laugh
to express her amazement. 'Your father's right. After this war, the lower orders are going to be
frightfully presumptuous.'

'Did you see the holes in the little one's pullover?' asked Sheila.

'I'm afraid I didn't see beyond their astonishing impudence,' replied her mother. She then was
55 aware that Roderick still remained in the corner. 'Roderick, come over to the fire at once. Your
jacket's wet through.' She became anxious as she saw how pale, miserable and pervious to
disease he looked. 'You'll be taking another of those wretched colds.'

He did not move.

'What's the matter?' she asked.

60 His response shocked her. He turned and pressed his brow against the window.

Questions

32. Summarise what happens in this extract from the novel. Make at least **three** key points.

3

33. Look at lines 1–8. Describe the relationship between Neil and Calum at this point in the novel, and with close reference to the text show how the writer uses language effectively to convey this relationship.

3

34. Look at lines 9–45. Show how any **two** examples of the writer's use of language contribute to a growing tension.

4

35. Look at lines 46–60. How does Roderick react to this incident and how does the writer's use of language convey this?

2

36. By referring to this extract, and to at least **two** other incidents from elsewhere in the novel, explain the importance of the character of Roderick to the novel as a whole.

8

SCOTTISH TEXT (POETRY)

If you choose to write on this text in Section A you may not write a critical essay on poetry in Section B.

Read the extract below and then attempt the following questions.

Text 1

Originally by Carol Ann Duffy

We came from our own country in a red room
which fell through the fields, our mother singing
our father's name to the turn of the wheels.
My brothers cried, one of them bawling Home,
5 Home, as the miles rushed back to the city,
the street, the house, the vacant rooms
where we didn't live any more. I stared
at the eyes of a blind toy, holding its paw.
All childhood is an emigration. Some are slow,
10 leaving you standing, resigned, up an avenue
where no one you know stays. Others are sudden.
Your accent wrong. Corners, which seem familiar,
leading to unimagined, pebble-dashed estates, big boys
eating worms and shouting words you don't understand.
15 My parents' anxiety stirred like a loose tooth
in my head. I want our own country, I said.
But then you forget, or don't recall, or change,
and, seeing your brother swallow a slug, feel only
a skelf of shame. I remember my tongue
20 shedding its skin like a snake, my voice
in the classroom sounding just like the rest. Do I only think
I lost a river, culture, speech, sense of first space
and the right place? Now, Where do you come from?
strangers ask. Originally? And I hesitate.

Questions

37. Show how **two** examples effectively evoke the experience of the persona leaving home.

4

38. Look at lines 9–16.

   (a) **In your own words**, explain some of the things that make the persona in the poem feel uncomfortable.

2

   (b) Explain how **one** example of language from these lines conveys this sense of discomfort.

2

39. How effective do you find the language of the last eight lines in conveying the idea of 'change'?

4

40. With close textual reference, show how the ideas and/or language of this poem are similar OR different to another poem or poems by Carol Ann Duffy that you have read.

8

If you choose to write on this text in Section A you may not write a critical essay on poetry in Section B.

Read the extract below and then attempt the following questions.

Text 2

***Divorce* by Jackie Kay**

I did not promise

to stay with you till death do us part, or

anything like that,

so part I must, and quickly. There are things

5   I cannot suffer

any longer: Mother, you never, ever said

a kind word

or a thank-you for all the tedious chores I have done;

Father, your breath

10 smells like a camel's and gives me the hump;

all you ever say is:

'Are you in the cream puff, Lady Muck?'

In this day and age?

I would be better off in an orphanage.

15 I want a divorce.

There are parents in the world whose faces turn

up to the light

who speak in the soft murmur of rivers

and never shout.

20 There are parents who stroke their children's cheeks

in the dead of night

and sing in the colourful voices of rainbows,

red to blue.

Those parents are not you. I never chose you.

25 You are rough and wild,

I don't want to be your child. All you do is shout

and that's not right.

I will file for divorce in the morning at first light.

Questions

41. **In your own words**, explain the reasons that the persona gives for wanting to divorce her parents. Make at least **three** key points.

3

42. Look at lines 1–14. Show how any **two** examples of the poet's use of language effectively conveys the persona's dissatisfaction with her parents.

4

43. Explain what kind of parents the persona imagines, then go on to show how the writer uses language effectively to describe these parents.

3

44. How effective do you find any aspect of the final five lines as a conclusion to the poem?

Your answer might deal with ideas and/or language.

2

45. With close textual reference, show how the ideas and/or language of this poem are similar OR different to another poem or poems by Jackie Kay that you have read.

8

If you choose to write on this text in Section A you may not write a critical essay on poetry in Section B.

Read the extract below and then attempt the following questions.

Text 3

Aunt Julia by Norman MacCaig

Aunt Julia spoke Gaelic

very loud and very fast.

I could not answer her –

I could not understand her.

5   She wore men's boots

when she wore any.

– I can see her strong foot,

stained with peat,

paddling with the treadle of the spinningwheel

10   while her right hand drew yarn

marvellously out of the air.

Hers was the only house

where I've lain at night

in the absolute darkness

15   of a box bed, listening to

crickets being friendly.

She was buckets

and water flouncing into them.

She was winds pouring wetly

20   round house-ends.

She was brown eggs, black skirts

and a keeper of threepennybits

in a teapot.

Aunt Julia spoke Gaelic

25 very loud and very fast.

By the time I had learned

a little, she lay

silenced in the absolute black

of a sandy grave

30 at Luskentyre.

But I hear her still, welcoming me

with a seagull's voice

across a hundred yards

of peatscrapes and lazybeds

35 and getting angry, getting angry

with so many questions

unanswered.

Questions

46. The first two stanzas of the poem establish the character of Aunt Julia and MacCaig's attitude to her.

   (a) Using your own words, summarise what Aunt Julia is like. Make at least **two** key points.

2

   (b) Show how the writer's use of language effectively conveys the character of Aunt Julia.

2

47. How do stanzas 3 and 4 develop the main ideas or concerns of the poem?

4

48. With close reference to the text, show how the poet's use of language in lines 24–37 make clear the feelings of the poet about Aunt Julia.

4

49. With close textual reference, show how the ideas and/or language of this poem are similar OR different to another poem or poems by Norman MacCaig that you have read.

8

If you choose to write on this text in Section A you may not write a critical essay on poetry in Section B.

Read the extract below and then attempt the following questions.

Text 4

Winter by Edwin Morgan

The year goes, the woods decay, and after,

many a summer dies. The swan

on Bingham's pond, a ghost, comes and goes.

It goes, and ice appears, it holds,

5   bears gulls that stand around surprised,

blinking in the heavy light, bears boys

when skates take over, the swan-white ice

glints only crystal beyond white. Even

dearest blue's not there, though poets would find it.

10   I find one stark scene

cut by evening cries, by warring air.

The muffled hiss of blades escapes into breath,

hangs with it a moment, fades off.

Fades off, goes, the scene, the voices fade,

15   the line of trees, the woods that fall, decay

and break, the dark comes down, the shouts

run off into it and disappear.

At last the lamps go too, when fog

drives monstrous down the dual carriageway

20   out to the west, and even in my room

and on this paper I do not know

about that grey dead pane

of ice that sees nothing and that nothing sees.

Questions

50. Look at lines 1–9. How does the poet's use of language in these lines help to clarify or illustrate the main ideas of the poem?

4

51. Look at lines 10–17. Show how any **two** examples of the poet's use of language in these lines effectively contribute to the main ideas or concerns of the poem.

4

52. Look at lines 18–23. Show how **two** examples of the writer's use of language help to create a sinister mood in these lines.

4

53. With close textual reference, show how the ideas and/or language of this poem are similar OR different to another poem or poems by Edwin Morgan that you have read.

8

Section B — Critical Essay — 20 marks

Write a critical essay on **one** question from this section of the exam paper. Select your question from **one** of the genres.

You can write on a Scottish text but **not** the same text you answered on in Section A of the exam. You must also write on a different **genre** to the one you selected in Section A.

You have approximately 45 minutes to complete your critical essay.

DRAMA

Your answer should refer closely to the text and to important elements such as characterisation, key scene(s), structure, climax, theme, plot, conflict, setting…

1. Choose a play in which the playwright portrays a central relationship that changes or develops.

   By referring to appropriate techniques, explain the nature of this relationship, then go on to show how the playwright portrays the development of this relationship.

2. Choose a play which explores a theme that made an impression on you.

   Explain briefly what the theme is then, by referring to appropriate techniques, show how the writer explores this theme.

PROSE

Your answer should refer closely to the text and to important elements such as characterisation, setting, language, key incident(s), climax, turning point, plot, structure, narrative technique, theme, ideas, description…

3. Choose a novel or a short story that creates mood or atmosphere effectively.

   By referring to appropriate techniques, show how the author has created this mood or atmosphere and how this influenced your response to the text.

4. Choose a novel or a short story or a work of non-fiction that made you consider an aspect of human nature or human society.

   By referring to appropriate techniques, describe the aspect of human nature or human society and then go on to discuss its importance to the text as a whole.

POETRY

Answers to questions in this part should refer to the text and to such relevant features as word choice, tone, imagery, structure, content, rhythm, rhyme, theme, sound, ideas…

5. Choose a poem that tells a story.

   Explain briefly what happens in the poem then show how the poet's telling of the story leads you to a deeper understanding of the poem's central concerns.

6. Choose a poem that has an important message for the reader.

   Explain briefly what this message is then, by referring to appropriate techniques, show how the poet explores this message.

FILM and TV DRAMA*

Answers to questions in this part should refer to the text and to such relevant features as use of camera, key sequence, characterisation, mise-en-scène, editing, setting, music/sound, special effects, plot, dialogue…

7. Choose a film or TV drama in which setting in a specific place is important.

   By referring to appropriate techniques, explain how the film or television makers depict the setting and explain why this is important to the effectiveness of the film.

8. Choose a film or TV drama that has a vital sequence.

   By referring to appropriate techniques, explain how the film or television makers make this sequence effective and why it is important to the play as a whole.

*'TV drama' includes a single play, a series or a serial.

LANGUAGE STUDY

Answers to questions in this part should refer to the text and to such relevant features as register, accent, dialect, slang, jargon, vocabulary, tone, abbreviation…

9. Consider how language differs between different generations.

   By referring to specific examples, describe some of these differences and why they are appropriate to each generation.

10. Consider how language is used in the media to report upon a specific area of activity such as sport, politics or celebrity.

By referring to specific examples, show how the language differs from Standard English and what advantages and/or disadvantages this offers for its speakers.

[END OF QUESTION PAPER]

Answers to Practice Exam A

WORKED ANSWERS — Practice Exam A

Reading for Understanding, Analysis and Evaluation

Question 1

Two of:

- Someone who has spent a lot of money to watch a famous team (1)
- Someone who is faithful to a small club (1)
- Someone who likes to feel they are important to the running of their favoured club (1)
- Someone who gets anxious and worried (1)
- Someone who watches to support a family member (1)

> **HINT** Look at the number of marks allocated to questions like this to see how many points you should make.

Question 2

Two of:

- 'centrepiece of their month' (1) – the focus of their thoughts (1)
- 'distracting' (1) – temporary, not fully involved (1)
- 'avoid weekend boredom' (1) – sense of avoiding worse alternatives (1)
- 'perspective' (1) – different standpoints are possible (1)
- 'unhealthily' (1) – damaging (1)
- 'obsessed' (1) – all encompassing, fanatical (1)

> **HINT** Remember to analyse your chosen quote as you will not receive full marks for simply quoting.

Question 3

Four of:

- People for whom looking forward to the event is the most important thing (1)
- People who love the drama (1)
- People who feel it is about being part of something bigger (1)
- People who imagine taking part (1)
- People who analyse tactics (1)
- People who follow the 'story' to find out how things will turn out, to be surprised (1)

> **HINT** When putting things into your own words, it does not always work to substitute word for word. Instead, make sure you convey the idea.

Question 4

One of:

- 'bloody good' (1) – informal language suggesting heat of argument (1)
- 'stimulates' (1) – excites strong emotions (1)
- 'challenges' (1) – forceful, stirring a strong response (1)
- 'provokes' (1) – inciting, inflaming (1)
- 'pugilistic' (1) – connection to boxing, physical confrontation (1)

Question 5

One of:

- Is too much money bad for sport?' (1)
    - Plus the effect of the question, which is to question the influence of excessive spending (1)
- 'Given they've got all these damned statistics, why do they keep picking the wrong team?' (1)
    - Plus the effect of the question, which is to question the use of data (1)
- 'If the standard of sport is improving, why do today's players seem less good than yesterday's giants?' (1)
    - Plus the effect of the question, which is to question whether modern athletes are better than those from the past (1)
- 'What part does luck play in top-class sport?' (1)
    - Plus the effect of the question, which is to question the importance of chance (1)

> **HINT** When presented with a choice, do not just choose the first one you see. Make sure that the example you have chosen will allow you to make detailed analysis.

Question 6

- Attitude – positive, favourable (1)
- 'Word choice – enjoyed'/'like music, literature or art'/'love it'/'deeper level' (1)

> **HINT** When you are asked about 'attitude' you must give an idea of how the writer **feels**.

Question 7

Three of:

- Shows how much lives are influenced by fortune (1)
- Gives ideas about how organisations can adapt and improve (1)
- Makes us think about difference between what we can see/prove and what we think/believe (1)
- Challenges the belief that everything was better in the past by showing how people constantly push barriers/make improvements (1)

Question 8

Four of:

- People with a temper find a way to be a part of something (1)
- Negative people find examples of things getting worse (1)
- Positive people find examples of things getting better (1)
- People who show understanding for others enjoy sport as if experiencing its highs and lows for themselves (1)
- Reasonable people don't understand why people don't think rationally about sport (1)

 HINT Structuring your answers in bullet points makes clear to you (and the marker) how many points you have made.

Question 9

The conclusion sums up some of the ideas of the passage. (1)

Evidence (one of):

- Mentioning 'fans' (1), 'prejudices' (1)
- It repeats the idea that sport is important (1)
- 'the unavoidable stuff of life' (1)/ 'a condensed version of life' (1)
- It finishes in a light-hearted / humorous tone (1)
- 'it matters less and comes up with better statistics' (1)

Question 10

Four of:

- Appeals to many different personalities (1)
- People get very involved and care about sport (1)
- Has wide and varied appeal (1)
- Can cause disputes (1)
- Can be experienced in very different ways (1)
- Can teach us lessons about life (1)

 HINT Re-read topic sentences, which are often the first sentence in each paragraph, to get an idea of the key ideas.

WORKED ANSWERS — Practice Exam A

Critical Reading, Section A: Scottish text

Drama, Text 1: *Bold Girls* **by Rona Munro**

Question 1

 HINT — Make your answer clear for questions like this. Bullet points or numbered lists are much clearer than a paragraph.

Three of:

- Domestic scene with lots of washing (1)
- There are lots of children's toys in various states (1)
- Messy (1)
- Worn furniture (1)
- There are signs of cooking (1)
- There are two pictures on the wall – one of the Virgin Mary (1) the other of Marie's deceased husband (1)

Question 2

Two of:

- Deirdre seems almost animalistic (1) – 'crouching on all fours' (1)
- Mysterious (1) – 'only her face is visible' (1)
- Dejected, unhappy (1) – repetition of 'grey' (1)

Question 3

 HINT — For 4-mark questions you should write a substantial answer. It is best to approach questions like this by giving four quotes with comments for 4 marks.

At least two of:

- Busy (1) – 'arms laden' (1)
- Bright (1) – 'cheerful' (1)
- Impatient (1) – 'No you cannot' (1)
- Constantly supplying food and drink (1) – *'four packets of crisps…biscuits'* (1)
- Resourceful (1) – 'starts two jobs simultaneously' (1)
- In control (1) – 'starts sorting' (1)
- Diligent (1) – 'frenetic efficiency' (1)

Question 4

General comment stating men are absent from the stage but have a massive influence on the female characters (1)

And one of:

- 'picture of the Virgin on one wall… smiling young man on the other' (1) – Michael's picture is seen next to the picture of the Virgin Mary. Marie idolises him and refuses to accept that he might have done anything wrong (1)
- 'Mickey were you wanting smoky bacon?' (1) – Marie is constantly providing for her children, as she does for Mickey (1)
- Use of the word 'bold' (1) meaning he is being cheeky/his behaviour is inappropriate (1)

Question 5

 HINT You need to show you understand the character of Deirdre and her influence on the other characters and relationships in the play. A successful answer will show an understanding of how Deirdre acts as a catalyst, making the others re-examine their lives.

You might refer to some of the following in your answer. However, there are other possibilities that you could discuss.

- Marie comes from outside, bringing truths that Marie has shut out of her life.
- Marie welcomes Deirdre into her home, attempting to look after her.
- Deirdre brings a knife, representing the violence which has shaped the women's lives and the society in which they live.
- Deirdre destroys Nora's material, shattering the peaceful domesticity.
- Deirdre wears Marie's wedding dress.
- Deirdre reveals that Marie's husband Michael, had several affairs, including one with Cassie, Marie's best friend.
- At the end Deirdre cares for Deirdre, making her breakfast.
- Marie tells Cassie – 'me and Michael always wanted a wee girl' and it seems that Deirdre becomes Marie's 'wee girl'.

Drama, Text 2: *Tally's Blood* by Anne-Marie di Mambro

Question 6

 HINT *Tally's Blood* is a long play. It would be helpful to give scenes titles to help you remember each one. You might call this scene, for example, 'The Attack on the Shop.'

At least three of:

- Massimo thinks back to Italy and says how much he misses home (1)
- Rosinella rushes in to warn him that a mob is coming to attack the shop (1)
- Lucia becomes frightened (1)
- She is reassured by first Rosinella and then Massimo (1)
- Lucia and Rosinella go in to rescue stock from the shop (1)

- The mob arrive, chanting racist abuse (1)
- The mob enter and vandalise the shop (1)
- Rosinella stops Massimo from confronting the mob (1)

Question 7

Two of:

- Repetition of 'bare' (1), showing the basic nature of the house (1)
- 'no water, no cludgie, no lights, no gas' (1) – emphasises the lack of amenities (1)
- 'walk two miles for water', 'a hole in the ground with a plank across it' (1) – primitive facilities (1)
- '(A beat)' (1) – pause to emphasise humour (1)
- 'God, I wish I was there now' (1) – contradicts everything that has gone before (1)

Question 8

You must name the mood or atmosphere. Then go on to focus in more detail on how the language conveys this mood.

Mood or atmosphere:

- Tense, frightening, suspenseful, nerve-racking… (1)

Writer's use of language (one of):

- 'ROSINELLA: (Screams) Massimo!' (1) – panic (1)
- 'Quick.' (1) – short sentence, urgency (1)
- Repetition of 'Quick.' (1) – emphasises panic, urgency (1)
- Rosinella's use of commands, e.g. 'You get the cigarettes…' (1) – she tries to take charge (1)
- 'Massimo! You don't think…surely?' (1) – fear, disbelief (1)
- 'Lucia starts to weep' (1) – terror (1)
- 'Get the Tallies!' etc. (1) – abuse from mob (1)

Question 9

One quotation may be enough if your comments are very detailed. It is better practice to include two quotations.

Rosinella

At least one of:

- Calls her 'my darling' (1) – shows affection (1)
- 'You're too wee…' (1) – tries to explain to Lucia/possibly shows a patronising or over-protective attitude towards her (1)

Massimo

OR at least one of:

- 'Massimo in: Lucia runs to him' (1) – Lucia adores him (1)
- 'It's alright darling' (1) – reassuring (1)
- 'So long as they leave you two alone.' (1) – protective (1)

Question 10

You might refer to some of the following in your answer. However, there are other possibilities that you could discuss.

- At this point in the play, the pressures on Massimo make him long for a return to Italy.
- The play begins with Rosinella and Massimo having to leave Italy in secret.
- In Scotland, Massimo works extremely hard to make his business a success.
- Throughout the novel the characters use Scots dialect, suggesting they have integrated linguistically.
- Rosinella does not approve of Scottish suitors for Lucia, specifically Hughie.
- Massimo reflects on the problems caused by the war in a long speech in scene 14.
- When the family return to Italy they no longer seem to fit in, in particular Lucia.
- The final words of the play show the mixture of influences on the characters: 'Stuff to keep us going. Bread, salami, cheese…Lots of ginger.'

Drama, Text 3: *Sailmaker* by Alan Spence

Question 11

Four of:

- Alec criticises his father for drinking too much (1)
- Davie has spent time with a woman, which Alec resents (1)
- Alec confronts Davie about being attracted to the woman (1)
- Davie hits Alec (1)
- The house is cold because Davie has not bought any coal (1)
- At the end of the extract Alec retrieving the yacht from the Glory Hole seems to bring father and son together (1)

Question 12 (a)

One of:

- feels sorry for himself (1) – 'It's no easy on your own' (1)
- struggles to face the reality of their situation (1) – 'ah need a wee break once in a while' (1)
- Davie does not take charge of things, procrastinates (1) – 'Ah'll get some themorra' (1)
- Davie bursts into anger (1) – '*slaps him, exits*' (1)

Question 12 (b)

One of:

- angry at his father (1) – 'So ye go and get bevvied…' (1)
- seems bitter (1) – '(Sarcastic) The really nice person' (1)
- regretful (1) – 'I keep goin back.' (1)
- Confused (1) – 'What is it I'm tryin to remember?' (1)
- Nostalgic (1) – 'd'ye remember that poem…?' (1)

Question 13

 The stage directions in *Sailmaker* are very important. They give indications about staging and also give clear insights into the characters' emotions.

Two of:

- *'Sarcastic'* (1) – shows the bitterness in his voice (1)

- *'Davie slaps him, exits'* (1) – sudden, unexpected, shows how difficult relationship has become (1)

- *'Darkness. Spotlight on Alec.'* (1) – shifts to Alec's monologue (1)

- *'Davie…staring into empty hearth'* (1) – shows the lack of warmth in relationship, the loss of Davie's hope (1)

Question 14

You might refer to some of the following in your answer. However, there are other possibilities that you could discuss.

- Alec's speech '… Sometimes in the middle of the night,' refers back to the opening of the play and shows how Alec and Davie have been affected by the death of Alec's mother.

- When Alec says 'I actually thought you wrote it' shows how he looked up to his father.

- Alec retrieving the yacht is a reminder of how often Davie has promised, and failed, to fix it up for his son.

- The yacht is subsequently destroyed, marking a final breakdown in Alec and Davie's relationship.

- Also, it is possible to refer to other father/son relationship in the play, between Ian and his father, Billy.

 Make sure that, before you begin discussing the rest of the play, you clearly state what is important about the extract provided.

Prose, Text 1: *The Crater* by Iain Crichton Smith

Question 15

 A lot of events are packed into this extract. There is no harm in picking out more than three key events.

At least three of:

- Robert decides they must rescue the soldier (1)

- They run because there is no reason to crawl/they have to rush (1)

- They check several craters (1)

- They hear him at the final crater (1)

- They call to him (1)

- He hears and moves towards them (1)

- Robert holds his rifle into the crater (1)

- The trapped soldier takes hold of the rifle (1)

- The other soldiers hold onto Robert (1)

- They pull him out of the crater (1)

- The soldier who was trapped dies (1)

Question 16

Mood or atmosphere:

- Tense, suspenseful, terrifying, horrific, bleak etc. (1)

Writer's use of language (one of):

- Short, abrupt sentences (e.g. 'The splashings came closer') (1) – sense of panic, desperation, speed of actions…(1)
- Onomatopoeia (e.g. 'bubbling', 'splashings') (1) – reader is made aware of sounds that Robert is desperately listening for (1)
- 'They cried fiercely' (1) – desperate, upset, frightened (1)
- 'The voice was like an animal's' (1) – simile, dehumanises trapped soldier (1)
- 'a great fish' (1) – simile, dehumanising soldier (1)
- 'For Christ's sake' (1) – cursing, anxiety (1)
- Repetition: 'breathing, frantic breathing' (1) – focus on vital signs of life (1)
- 'It wasn't right that a man should die in green slime' (1) – Robert's voice, determination not to fail (1)
- 'And…'/'But…' at the start of sentences (1) – sense of panic, speed…(1)
- 'Was it Morrison down there after all?' (1) – Robert's thoughts, questioning own actions, suggesting futility (1)

Question 17

> Using sub-headings here helps to indicate to the marker that you are dealing with more than one technique.

Two of:

Word choice:

- 'it' (1) – dehumanises the soldier, makes him seem strange, unrecognisable, frightening…(1)
- 'stench' (1) – horrible smell (1)
- 'mottled' (1) – seems decayed, damaged (1)
- 'hung there' (1) – desperate (1)
- 'teeth gritted' (1) – determined (1)

Repetition:

- 'it' (1) – dehumanises (1)
- 'cheering' (1) – emphasises sense of relief, joy (1)

Simile:

- 'like a disease' (1) – death, infection, something to fear (1)
- 'as if up a mountainside' (1) – difficulty (1)
- 'It was like a body which might have come from space, green and illuminated and shiny' (1) – seems alien, strange, frightening (1)

Climax:

- 'the face…the teeth…the mouth…got him over the side' (1) – creates suspense, doubt (1)

Question 18

 Your answer should show the disappointment that despite Robert's efforts the soldier has died.

Any two of:

- The soldier dies when it seemed he had been saved (1)
- 'at that moment' shows the sudden realisation (1)
- 'He's dead' – matter-of-fact tone (1)
- Contrast with the excitement of 'cheering' (1)

Question 19

 The Crater, like two of the other stories in the collection (*In Church* and *The Telegram*), deals with war. However, a really strong answer will also link the story to the other stories.

You might refer to some of the following in your answer. However, there are other possibilities that you could discuss.

- This story depicts the brutality of war, through an almost hallucinatory experience.
- The closest parallels are with the story *In Church;* both of these stories shockingly illustrate the cruelty of war.
- *The Telegram* could also be discussed, showing the impact of war on the home front.
- Crichton Smith's characterisation in these stories could also be discussed. It would be interesting to compare, for example, Sergeant Smith's apparent callousness to the depiction of the mothers in *The Telegram* and the villagers in *The Painter*.

Prose, Text 2: *Dear Santa* by Anne Donovan

Question 20

At least three of:

- Alison makes several failed attempts at beginning her letter (because she wants to ask Santa to make her mother love her more) (1)
- Alison's mother comes into her bedroom and encourages Alison to finish her letter (1)
- Alison writes a letter, asking for toys (1)
- Alison's mother tucks Alison into bed (1)
- Alison asks her mother why her hair is a different colour (1)
- Alison's mother kisses Alison and says good night (1)

Question 21

 HINT The narrator does not state her feelings explicitly, but various techniques – questions, word choice – are used to show her irritation.

Mood or atmosphere:

Uncertain, frustrated (1)

Writer's use of language (one of):

- 'It's hard tae find the words' (1) – finding it hard to express herself (1)
- Incomplete, failed attempts (1) – 'Please could you' (1)
- Questions (1) – 'But what is it ah'm tryin tae say?' (1)
- 'That's no Santa's job' (1) – becoming upset (1)
- 'there's nae point' (1) – loses heart, feels it is futile (1)
- 'If there is a Santa' (1) – doubt (1)
- 'the sky's dirty grey' (1) – sad, gloomy (1)

Question 22

Any combination of two bullet points for four marks

Relationship – strained, distant:

- 'Are you no asleep yet?' (1) – impatience (1)
- 'Look, there's Katie, soond' (1) – unfavourable comparison to sister (1)
- 'she cannae be bothered wi that' (1) – irritation (1)
- 'a dry kiss, barely grazin ma cheek' (1) – lack of affection (1)

Relationship – Alison's affection for mother:

- 'Ah love stroking her hair' (1) – touchy-feely (1)
- 'ah wisht ah had hair like yours' (1) – admires mother (1)

Question 23

 HINT The words 'in your opinion' make clear that you must give your own response here. You must also back up this response with evidence as no marks are awarded for merely stating your opinion.

Alison feels content, happy (one of):

- 'she looks at me mair soft like' (1) Alison's mother has mellowed (1)
- 'leavin a wee crack of light fallin across the bedclothes' (1) – positive imagery of 'light', thoughtful act (1)

OR

Alison feels disappointed (one of):

- 'Go tae sleep hen…' – mother still impatient (1)
- 'a dry kiss, barely grazin ma cheek' – lack of affection (1)

Question 24

 HINT A strong answer here will deal not only with the similarity of the characters and relationships but also the use of techniques like narrative voice.

You might refer to some of the following in your answer. However, there are other possibilities that you could discuss.

- This story, like *All That Glisters,* deals with miscommunication between the generations: here a young girl feels a lack of affection from her mother.
- The story *Away in a Manger* also features a mother and daughter.
- The Christmas setting is also similar to *Away in a Manger.*
- *A Chitterin Bite* deals with the difference between children and adults by looking at the same character during childhood and adulthood.
- *Virtual Pals* also deals with miscommunication.
- The use of Scots in both dialogue and the first person narrator's voice is similar to *All That Glisters..*

Prose, Text 3: *The Testament of Gideon Mack* by James Robertson

Question 25

 HINT Annotating the extract can help you to see clearly how the plot progresses.

At least three of:

- Gideon and his father watch *Batman* together (1)
- Gideon's father becomes extremely angry (1)
- Gideon's mother comes in and asks for an explanation (1)
- Gideon's father collapses (with a stroke) (1)
- Gideon goes to the telephone to call an ambulance (1)

Question 26

Mood/atmosphere:

Embarrassed, ashamed, awkward, uncomfortable (1)

Writer's use of language (any two):

- 'It felt like an hour' (1) – uneasiness (1)
- 'squirmed' (1) – sense of shame (1)
- Repetition of 'hated' (1)
- 'I saw it through his eyes' (1) – guilt at disobeying father (1)
- Series of critical adjectives, showing how Gideon now judges the programme (1) – 'cheap, tawdry, meaningless' (1)
- 'cheap' (1) – low quality (1)
- 'tawdry' (1) – tasteless (1)

- 'meaningless' (1) – empty (1)

- 'rubbish' (1) – disposable, waste of time (1)

Question 27

 HINT Avoid vague answers to questions such as this such as, 'His father is not happy.' Be specific: 'The word "creeping" suggests that his father feels Gideon has been sneaking around behind his back. His father feels Gideon is deceptive.'

Two of:

- 'Do not interrupt me' (1) – command, anger, taking control (1)

- 'drivel' (1) – nonsense (1)

- 'unutterable garbage'/'trash' (1) – rubbish (1)

- 'feel the storm coming' (1) – metaphor, Gideon weak in the face of father's fury (1)

- 'muttering into a mighty wind' (1) – Gideon is overpowered, his father is like a force of nature (1)

- 'creeping' (1) – feels Gideon was deceptive, sneaking (1)

- 'skulking'/'taken your sin into a corner to play with' (1) – secretive (1)

- 'wallowing in that filth' (1) – disgust (1)

- 'disgraced' (1) – feels let down (1)

- 'sullied' (1) – Gideon has committed a sin (1)

- 'makes me sick' (1) – physical reaction (1)

Question 28

One of:

- Repetition of 'something' (1) – uncertainty (1)

- 'quivering' (1) – contrast with James Mack's previous strength (1)

- 'crumpled in a heap' (1) – weak (1)

- 'folding like a collapsible ruler' (1) – contrast with previous strength (1)

- 'stood there like a statue' (1) – immobile (1)

- Short, imperative sentences, e.g. 'Phone…Dial…' (1) – urgency (1)

- Short final sentence (1) – 'I ran to the telephone' (1)

Question 29

 HINT You need to show understanding of how the relationship between Gideon and James Mack changes and develops as the story progresses. Focus on key points in their relationship. You might refer to some of the following in your answer. However, there are other possibilities that you could discuss.

The influence of Gideon's father is felt throughout the novel:

- James Mack is a controlling influence, forcing on Gideon a strict religious upbringing; on the first page of Gideon's narration he describes himself as 'a dutiful wee boy growing up in the shadow of his father and of the Kirk'

- Gideon does credit James with instilling qualities in him: 'how to think, how to argue…'

- The television, which is key to the extract, is brought into the home because of James' passion for football. This hints at other desires that are suppressed

- Gideon rebels against his father by secretly watching (particularly American) television programmes

- It could be argued that Gideon's upbringing influences his own relationships, which often seem distant and lack affection: 'There was ice built around my heart'

- Gideon follows his father into the ministry

- After his meeting with the Devil, Gideon views his father differently. Gideon comes to believe that James was scarred by his experience of war

Prose, Text 4: *Kidnapped* by Robert Louis Stevenson

Question 30

 HINT   This extract is full of action, but do not neglect the insights into character, which are also provided.

At least four of:

- The seamen attack the roundhouse (1)

- Balfour overcomes his fear and shoots two of the attackers (1)

- Breck fights them off with his cutlass (1)

- Breck hugs Balfour (1)

- Breck boasts of his fighting ability (1)

- Breck stabs the dead and wounded attackers to make sure they are dead (1)

- Breck sings (1)

Question 31

One of:

- 'my whole flesh misgave me' (1) – initially in shock (1)

- 'either my courage came again, or I grew so much afraid' (1) – stirred to action (1)

- 'I might have stood and stared at them' (1) – again David is stunned into inaction (1)

- 'brought me to my senses' (1) – acts to help Breck (1)

Question 32

Two of:

- 'roaring…scream…roaring' (1) – noise (1)

- 'the most horrible, ugly groan' (1) – pain, Balfour's shock (1)

- 'tumbled in a lump' (1) – untidy, confusion (1)

- 'the fellow clung like a leech' (1) – desperation (1)
- 'ran upon the others like a bull' (1) – strength (1)
- 'They broke before him like water' (1) – easily overcome by Breck (1)
- 'The sword in his hands flashed like quicksilver' (1) – speed and skill (1)
- 'turning, and running, and falling one against another' (1) – confusion of battle (1)
- 'driving them along the deck as a sheep-dog chases sheep' (1) – supremacy of Breck (1)

Question 33

One of:

- 'I love you like a brother' (1) – loyal, affectionate (1)
- 'am I no a bonny fighter?' (1) – boastful (1)

Question 34

> The relationship between Breck and Balfour is one of the central interests in the novel. You need to convey how the relationship between David Balfour and Alan Breck changes as the story goes on.

You might refer to some of the following in your answer. However, there are other possibilities that you could discuss.

- Balfour feels he should assist Breck as he too is betrayed.
- The two have different allegiances: Balfour is pro-Whig while Breck is a Jacobite. Breck must overcome his initial suspicion of Balfour.
- At times Balfour becomes frustrated by Breck, at one point calling him a 'treacherous child'.
- The two go on the run together, Breck's knowledge of the glens and experience in fighting helping Balfour to survive. He also uses his contacts to protect Balfour, e.g. convincing Cluny to look after him.
- Breck helps Balfour to his rightful inheritance in the climax of the novel.

Prose, Text 5: *The Cone-Gatherers*

Question 35

At least three of:

- Calum chases after the deer (1)
- One of the deer is shot and wounded (1)
- Calum holds the wounded deer (1)
- Duror rushes to the wounded deer and Calum (1)
- Duror uses a knife to put the deer out of its misery (1)
- Duror becomes so covered in blood that the others suspect he has been killed (1)
- The others – Tulloch, Graham, Lady Runcie-Campbell – catch up with Duror (1)
- Graham drags away the dead deer (1)

Question 36

Here, and throughout the novel, Calum has a connection with the natural world/is at home in nature/feels empathy with animals (1).

OR

This extract suggests that nature can be cruel/that death is a part of nature (1)

AND

- 'his cry was of delight and friendship' (1) – immediate, instinctive reaction; happiness and kinship (1)
- 'marvellous grace and agility' (1) – beauty (1)
- 'flew for the doom ahead' (1) – inevitability of death (1)
- 'he too was a deer' (1) – Calum's connection with nature (1)
- 'not...so swift or sure of foot' (1) – Calum/mankind is divided from nature (1)
- 'the indifference of all nature' (1) – uncaring (1)

Question 37

Two of:

- 'The dogs barked fiercely' – threat and violence (2)
- 'commotion...resounded...bellowed loudest' – noise and confusion (2)
- 'hopped...sprang forward' – action and anxiety (2)
- 'as Neil had vehemently warned him' – Neil's fears realised (2)
- 'with wails of lament, he dashed on at demented speed' – Calum's panic (2)
- 'screaming in sympathy' – Calum's despair (2)
- 'Lady Runcie-Campbell stood petrified' – frozen with terror (2)

Question 38

Two of:

'Duror bawled to his dogs to stop lest they interfere with the shooting' – shows he wants killing to continue (1)

- 'laughing in some kind of berserk joy' – demonstrates bizarre delight in cruelty (1)
- 'furious force' – shows he is possessed by anger, violence (1)
- 'seizing. . .savagely' – violence (1)
- 'Duror had the appearance of a drunk man...' – shows Duror's loss of control, intoxicated by violence (1)

Question 39

You might refer to some of the following in your answer. However, there are other possibilities that you could discuss.

- This extract depicts a vital stage in Duror's descent into evil.
- Even at the beginning of the novel, Duror harbours a passionate hatred for Calum; Jenkins describes him observing Calum in an 'icy sweat of hatred' in the first chapter.

- Jenkins depicts how Duror appears to focus his resentment at having to care for his wife on Calum: 'Since childhood Duror had been repelled by anything living that had an imperfection or deformity or lack'.

- Duror has deliberately arranged for Neil and Calum to be part of the hunt to torture them.

- Duror's terrifying appearance in this extract is one description of several which shows the manifestation of evil.

- Duror continues to plot against Calum, telling Lady Runcie-Campbell that Calum is evil.

- Duror resists the doctor's attempts to help: 'he felt in a mood for murder, rape, or suicide'.

- The climactic murder of Calum.

Poetry, Text 1: *Anne Hathaway* by Carol Ann Duffy

Question 40

> *HINT*   You need to make two distinct comments to get the two marks.

Two of:

- The relationship was loving (1)

- Anne admired her husband's talent (1)

- Anne provided inspiration for Shakespeare (1)

- Shakespeare has died and she misses him (1)

- The bed, although 'second best' is a way for Anne to remember her husband (1)

Question 41

Two of:

- 'a spinning world' (1) – their imaginations meant that this small space contained a huge amount of ideas and stories (1)

- Series of locations, 'forests, castles…' (1) – shows that he made her feel she had experienced many fascinating places (1)

- 'torchlight' (1) – mystery (1)

- 'dive for pearls' (1) – adventure, precious moments together (1)

Question 42

Two of:

- 'My lover's words' (1) – importance of Shakespeare's talent to Anne (1)

- 'were shooting stars' (1) – heavenly, fleeting, magical (1)

- Series of words related to literature and language (1) – 'words…rhyme…assonance… verb…noun' (1)

- 'Some nights, I dreamed he'd written me' (1) – Anne shares her husband's imagination/feels that he has created her (1)

- 'by touch, by scent, by taste' (1) – sensuousness of language (1)

Question 43

 Think what the term 'conclusion' means. Is this a summary of the ideas? Does the language make a link to earlier in the poem?

One of:

- 'the other bed' (1) – refers back to the epigraph, showing that this is the bed that has sentimental significance (1)
- 'our guests dozed on' (1) – contrasts with imaginative adventures (1)
- 'living laughing love' (1) – alliteration, lives on for Anne, fun (1)
- 'hold him in the casket' (1) – retains her memory of Shakespeare (1)
- 'he held me' (1) – intimacy (1)

Question 44

 Your answer should be supported by detailed quotations from the poems being discussed. On their own, however, quotations will not get you marks. Make obvious the way that the quotes connect to this poem.

You might refer to some of the following in your answer. However, there are other possibilities that you could discuss.

- Like *Valentine* the poem uses one strong central symbol to explore the theme of love.
- Finds inspiration from literature like *Havisham*.
- Seeks to understand the wife of a famous figure like *Mrs Midas*.
- Contrasts with a different view of a creative process in *War Photographer*.

Poetry, Text 2: *Bed* by Jackie Kay

Question 45 (a)

Two of:

- feeling like a liability to her daughter (1)
- restricted mobility (1)
- feeling like she has become her daughter's child (1)
- not communicating with her daughter as much (1)

Question 45 (b)

 There are plenty of examples to choose from here. Make sure your answer does enough to get four marks.

Two of:

- 'burden' (1) – literally a weight, a difficulty (1)
- 'Stuck here' (1) – frustration (1)

- 'blastit bed' (1) – alliteration, as if she is spitting out the words (1)
- 'things she has tae dae…' (1) – sense of guilt (1)
- 'champed egg…mashed tattie' (1) – childish foods, making mother feel inadequate (1)
- 'A dinny ken…' (1) – lack of understanding (1)
- 'plucked oot o us' (1) – painful, forced (1)

Question 46

Two of:

- 'like some skinny chicken' (1) – simile, showing her unpleasant appearance (1)
- '(an yet…guid smooth skin)' (1) – parenthesis to show her wistfully remembering her youth (1)
- 'A've seen hale generations…' (1) – awareness of her restricted life, nostalgia for past (1)
- 'no seen a lick o paint fir donkeys' (1) – rundown state of window, mirrors woman's own physical deterioration (1)
- 'Kerrs…Campbells' (1) – lost sense of community (1)
- 'no seen ony Campbell in a long time' (1) – sense of isolation (1)
- 'the great heaving sigh' (1) – disappointment (1)
- 'ma crabbit tut' (1) – ill-tempered (1)
- 'Am just bidin time so am ur' (1) – sense of waiting for death (1)

Question 47

One of:

- 'Time is whit A'hauld…' (1) – remaining time is limited (1)
- 'the skeleton' (1) – death (1)
- 'glaring selfish moon' (1) – sense of insignificance (1)
- 'how wull she feel?'/'No that Am saying A want her guilty'/'No that Am saying Am no grateful' (1) – strained relationship with daughter (1)

Question 48

> **HINT**   Whether you choose to write in paragraphs or developed bullet points, a structured approach will help you get marks, for example, using a SEE structure: Statement of similarity to another poem, Evidence (quote), Explanation of the importance of this quote.

You might refer to some of the following in your answer. However, there are other possibilities that you could discuss.

- All of the Jackie Kay poems in the selection explore family relationships.
- *Lucozade* provides the closest comparison, describing the same relationship from the point of view of the daughter. The direct speech of the mother in *Lucozade* – 'Where's the big brandy…the biscuit tin, the chocolate gingers' – provides particularly interesting points for comparison.
- The poem *Divorce* also looks at a strained relationship between mother and daughter, with an interesting contrast in *Divorce*'s use of the voice of the child.

- *Gap Year* expands upon the distance between mother and daughter and muses on the passing of time, with more nostalgia than bitterness: 'A flip and a skip ago, you were dreaming in your basket'.

Poetry, Text 3: *Sounds of the Day* by Norman MacCaig

Question 49 (a)

Two of:

- horses' hooves (1)
- birds (1)
- water/waves (1)
- a waterfall (1)

Question 49 (b)

> Choose your quotations carefully. Because MacCaig wants to emphasise the sounds in the poem he uses the same techniques repeatedly. However, you should try not to repeat yourself in your answer.

Two of:

- 'clatter came' (1) – onomatopoeia, alliteration (1)
- 'air creaked' (1) – onomatopoeia (1)
- 'seeing us off the premises' (1) – personification (1)
- 'snuffling puff' (1) – onomatopoeia (1)
- 'blocking, unblocking' (1) – repeated action (1)
- 'black drums rolled' (1) – evokes the rumble of the waterfall (1)

Question 50

Four of:

- Two short stanzas, contrasting with longer first stanza (1)
- Shift from description of natural world to domestic – 'door', 'fire' (1) or from outside to inside – 'door scraped shut' (1)
- 'the end of all the sounds there are' – silence, contrasting with the sounds described in the first stanza (1)
- Use of 'you' – direct address (1)
- 'me' – poem becomes more personal (1)
- 'the quietest fire in the world' – silence, emphasised by superlative (1)

Question 51

One of:

> Your answer must give a sense of what 'an effective conclusion' is. It can do this by showing how ideas in this stanza link to those from previous lines or how it leaves a lasting impression on the reader.

- 'you…your…you' (1) – again, directly addressing the reader (1)
- 'freezing water' (1) – links to the water of the first stanza/describes shock of grief (1)
- 'a bangle of ice' (1) – feeling compared to something physical/sensual like sounds of the first 9 lines (1)
- 'the whole hand goes numb' (1) – sorrow, ending the poem by expressing grief (1)

Question 52

You might refer to some of the following in your answer. However, there are other possibilities that you could discuss.

- The poem *Memorial* also deals with grief and the persona's attempts to come to terms with mourning: 'Everywhere she dies.' In doing so, the poem also evokes the natural world.
- *Visiting Hour* describes the persona visiting his wife in hospital and his struggle to come to terms with her illness.
- *Aunt Julia* treats the theme of mortality.
- *Assissi* also uses contrast to great effect and describes the sounds of the incident described.

Poetry, Text 4: *Hyena* by Edwin Morgan

Question 53 (a)

Two of:

- threatening (1)
- desperate (1)
- starving (1)
- frightening (1)
- callous (1)

Question 53 (b)

> Make sure your analysis of quotations does not simply restate your answer for 1(a). The answers should be more specific to the quotations you have chosen.

Two of:

- 'I am waiting for you' (1) – direct, menace (1)
- 'I have…not eaten'/'I found no water hole' (1) – details of hardship (1)
- 'You must believe I am prepared to spring' (1) – constant danger (1)
- 'a rough coat like Africa' (1) – suited to the difficult conditions of the continent (1)
- 'a shuggy bundle of gathered energy' (1) – ready to strike (1)
- 'I trot, I lope, I slaver' (1) – series of verbs, conveying the behaviour of the hyena (1)

Question 54

> *HINT*   Make clear exactly what these 'main ideas of the poem' are.

Two of:

- 'Do you like my song?' (1) – hyena seems to seek approval (1)
- 'my song…I sing' (1) – musical (1)
- 'the moon pours hard and cold' (1) – the harshness of the environment (1)
- 'I am the slave of darkness' (1) – metaphor, evoking sympathy (1)
- 'I am a good match for a dead lion' (1) – equal to the 'king of the jungle' (1)
- 'a crowd of fangs' (1) – intimidating (1)
- 'I am not laughing. But I am not snarling either' (1) – hyena is not evil, only doing what is necessary to survive (1)

Question 55

One of:

- 'I am waiting' (1) – repeating first words of poem/threat (1)
- Repetition of 'for…' (1) – hyena will seize on any opportunity (1)
- 'For the leaping sinews to go slack' (1) – preying on weakness (1)
- 'I am crouching…till you are ready' (1) – addresses reader, suggesting our shared mortality (1)
- 'pick you clean and leave your bones' (1) – cold, callous (1)

Question 56

You might refer to some of the following in your answer. However, there are other possibilities that you could discuss.

- The harshness of nature is also portrayed in *Winter,* which paints a 'stark scene' closer to home.
- *Slate* also deals with mortality and nature.
- The poem *Trio* would provide an interesting contrast: while *Hyena* depicts a harsh environment where death seems inevitable, the festive cheer described in *Trio* resists the 'monsters of the year'.

WORKED ANSWERS — Practice Exam A

Critical Reading

Section B: Critical Essay

DRAMA

1. Most plays build to a climax and the main challenge of this question is to show how the climax is achieved dramatically. If possible, you should identify how elements such as stage directions and lighting contribute to the climax, e.g. Tennessee Williams' use of music in scene 9 of *A Streetcar Named Desire*. Shakespeare's plays do not provide plentiful stage directions so you should focus on the language and its effect on the

audience. For example, in *Othello* the title character's monologue over the sleeping body of Desdemona adds to the tension and also has thematic significance. It is vital not to slip into simply retelling the plot here – the focus must remain on the climax itself.

> **HINT** Make sure you identify clearly what the climax is at the beginning of your essay.

2. There are many plays that you could use here. The title character of *Macbeth,* like many tragic heroes, begins as an admirable character but descends into violence and cruelty. Techniques such as Shakespeare's use of soliloquy give us an insight into Macbeth's motivation and turmoil. A character who gains our approval as the play progresses is John Proctor in Arthur Miller's *The Crucible.* Minor characters such as Proctor's wife, Goody, might also be possibilities. However, you must make sure that you choose a character who changes or develops.

> **HINT** It is vitally important to keep the focus on **our** attitude to the character here. Using words and phrases like 'we' and 'the audience' regularly make sure that you are writing about our emotional response, e.g. 'We admire the character.'

PROSE

3. It is vital that you identify what the setting is in the introduction to your answer. You can then go on to discuss how this setting is described in detail. *The Great Gatsby* evokes 1920s New York; *The Strange Case of Dr Jekyll and Mr Hyde* does the same for Victorian London. What you must remember is to show the thematic significance of these settings: the symbolic importance of the settings in *Gatsby,* the way the foggy London of *Jekyll and Hyde* mirrors the way that desires and actions are hidden. There are many interesting non-fiction possibilities here too, such as the essays in Kathleen Jamie's collections *Findings* and *Sightlines.*

> **HINT** The question says 'setting in time and/or place'. It is very important when you have a choice like this that **you** clarify at the beginning of your essay which aspect you are dealing with, or whether you will deal with both. You need to be clear and you must communicate this to the marker.

4. This question is rather vague. It is your job to be specific: what is the theme and why is it relevant? The theme may be one of importance to society, e.g. crime in *On the Sidewalk Bleeding.* Or you may choose a text that deals with a theme with more personal significance such as *Me and Ma Gal* or *Mary Moon and the Stars'* depiction of friendship.

> **HINT** Make sure that you evaluate throughout your essay, showing how the writer's depiction of theme has an effect on **you**, the reader.

POETRY

5. Poetry often reflects upon the passing of time. First of all you should state clearly how time passes in your chosen poem: is it the passing of seasons? A child growing up? Shakespeare's sonnets often reflect on ageing and Sonnet 19 ('Devouring time…') in particular would be an excellent choice here. There are a huge number of options, from *Ozymandias* by Shelley to *On Craigie Hill* by Stewart Conn. The question specifically states that you must look at the 'use of poetic techniques' so you should look at how imagery, word choice, structure and so on communicate a difficult theme to the reader.

> **HINT** The list of techniques in the text box can be a handy reminder of aspects of the poem you can discuss.

6. Emotion, of course, is vital to successful poetry. After a brief initial outline of what the poem is about you should focus clearly on **your** response. It is really important that you engage with the poem and make clear how you feel about the poem. A genuine emotional response will really impress the marker.

> **HINT** Make sure when you are studying and revising poetry that you do not just get lost in the detail. You need to step back and think what feelings the poet is trying to convey and try to engage with the poem on an emotional level.

FILM and TV DRAMA

7. When studying film and TV drama it is important to have a really firm grasp of the opening sequence. The opening should give the viewer a clear idea of the main characters, setting and genre. It is also likely that the central conflict or complication will be introduced during this sequence. Films such as *The Shawshank Redemption* and *Saving Private Ryan* have particularly arresting opening sequences.

8. Films in the crime or thriller genre provide rich pickings for questions like this. Gangster films often depict how crime can be seductive. There are many TV crime series that would be suitable too, such as *Broadchurch*. Films in the war genre would provide material for this question. There are also TV series such as the drama *Boy A*. The focus for this question is likely to be characterisation and a good answer would show how the characters' conflicts exemplify the theme.

LANGUAGE STUDY

9. To answer a question such as this, it is vital to study the language in detail. You may think that you are familiar with the language of, e.g. text messaging, but you will need to analyse the language in detail and show an awareness of technical terminology. However, with work, this would be an interesting and rich source for writing, looking at, e.g. the use of deviant spellings, abbreviations etc.

10. We are confronted with adverts constantly. To write a full essay about an advert, however, may present certain challenges. Most adverts are, by their nature, short. Therefore you would need to have a lot of examples at your fingertips to go into sufficient depth. With close study though, the use of comparatives and superlatives, imperative sentences, adjectives etc. would make for an interesting essay.

Answers to Practice Exam B

WORKED ANSWERS — Practice Exam B

Reading for Understanding, Analysis and Evaluation

Question 1 (a)

 There are two different examples here: the writer's own experience and the observations of Mathias Osvath. Make sure you look at both. Also, look at the details of the chimps' behaviour, explaining the stages of their behaviour and Osvath's findings about it.

Four of:

- Pretend disinterest (1)
- Make people come to look at them (1)
- Then throw faeces at the visitors for amusement (1)
- Santino could think ahead – 'plan for the future' (1)
- Collected things to throw before there were any people to throw them at (1)
- Able to create image of things still to come (1)

HINT

When you see a question that is split into two parts – (a) and (b) – you should read both parts before you begin to answer question (a). The questions will be related and will refer to the same section of the passage. Reading both parts of the question first makes sure you don't repeat yourself in your answers.

Question 1 (b)

 To get 4 marks for this question you must choose two quotes and analyse what these quotes suggest about the chimpanzee's behaviour. When analysing quotes, it is a good idea to say what the word/s **mean** and then what they **suggest**.

Two of:

- 'wily' (1) – suggests they are cunning, scheming, sneaky (1)
- 'rehearsed' (1) – practised, suggests they had worked together, improving their performance (1)
- 'nonchalance' (1) – (pretend) indifference, shows they were deceptive (1)
- 'complex' (1) – difficult, various parts to plan (1)
- 'methodically' (1) – carefully, logically, shows planning (1)

Question 2

HINT There are several possible answers here. For full marks, make sure you make four points and separate them clearly to indicate to the marker you have four answers.

Four of:

- Create utensils to make life easier (1)
- Show interest in naturally occurring spectacles (1)
- Become sad when other chimps die (1)

- Conduct conflicts with other chimps (1)

- Think ahead to kill other chimps (1)

- Show care for others (1)

- Seek comfort from others (1)

- Show signs of happiness/amusement (1)

- Make plans together (1)

- Make friendships (1)

- Pretend to trick others (1)

- Pretend for fun (1)

Question 3

 HINT These lines move from general statements – 'they grow into formidable beefcakes' – to a specific example about Carla Nash and Travis. The question is about chimpanzees in general so you should try to explain the point that the example illustrates.

Three of:

- They are incredibly powerful (1)

- It is difficult to know how they will act (1)

- They have the mentality of a child (1)

- The example of Travis shows that even chimpanzees who have been trained/are accustomed to their owners can act violently (1)

Question 4

 HINT There is a lot of information packed into this paragraph. To make sure you find two separate points, it may be helpful to highlight or underline key ideas in the passage.

Two of:

- Washoe acquired American Sign Language (1)

- Brought up as if he was a person (1)

- Learned a large number of signs (1)

- Became creative with use of language/found ways to explain unfamiliar things (1)

Question 5

 HINT For full marks here make sure that you focus on the **differences** between chimps and humans.

Two of:

- Humans have bigger brains (1)

- Our common ancestors date from a long time ago (1)

- We have evolved differently for a very long time (1)

Question 6

 HINT As the question asks you to 'explain' here you will not get marks for quoting. You should first try to explain the behaviour in your own words and then go on to make clear the link to human behaviour.

One of:

- Using sticks to catch insects/food (1), tools make our lives easier (1)

- Making a leaf into a cup (1), being creative with materials around us (1)

- Acting as if the chimp cannot see food so that other chimps are not attracted to it (1), deceiving others for our own gain (1)

- 'Cheating' on a partner secretly (1), being driven by sexual desire/not being faithful to partners (1)

Question 7

HINT Make sure that you clearly state a **feeling** here.

Feeling: uncomfortable, frightened, enlightened, sense of recognition (1)

Evidence (one of):

- 'a little bit of troglodyte in all of us' (1)

- 'unnerving' (1)

- 'look into the eyes' (1)

- 'closest relative' (1)

HINT

Sometimes candidates feel that they should start writing answers as soon as possible so do not read the passage thoroughly. This is a mistake. You should **read the whole passage** before you start answering. This will help you to get a clearer idea of the writer's main ideas and attitude to the topic and will help with your answers throughout.

Question 8

HINT Here you will only get full marks if you really analyse the image in detail. First, make sure you say what things are being compared and then say as much as you can about the ideas that this creates in the readers mind.

One of:

- 'chimps at London Zoo were able to construct mental pictures of the future' – comparison to drawing/painting, idea of creativity, clarity, detail…

- 'they grow into formidable beefcakes' – comparison to lump of meat/extremely muscled human, suggestion of lack of intelligence, strength, similarity to human, informality…

- 'when Washoe first saw a swan he made the signs for "water" and "bird", which…was like "getting an SOS from outer space".' – breakthrough is hugely significant, intelligent life found on Earth, link to science-fiction film relevant to film *Rise of the Planet of the Apes*…

(Full marks awarded for **full** and **detailed** analysis.)

Question 9

> Re-read notes you have made, sentences you have underlined and topic sentences to help you identify the **main ideas**. Do not get caught up in writing about specific examples, facts or statistics.

Four of:

- Chimps can make plans, predict future behaviour (1)
- Chimps are closely related to humans (1)
- Chimps use tools (1)
- Chimps show emotion (1)
- Chimps are very intelligent (1)
- Chimps can be dangerous (1)
- Chimps can develop language (1)
- There are significant differences between chimps and humans (1)
- Chimps are particularly similar in their use of cunning (1)

WORKED ANSWERS — Practice Exam B

Critical Reading, Section A: Scottish Text

Drama, Text 1: *Bold Girls* by Rona Munro

Question 1 (a)

Two of:

- 'a lovely man' (1) – appreciation of kindness (1)
- 'Gentle' (1) – affection (1)
- 'hold you in his lap like you had fur' (1) – care (1)
- 'ever stirred her daddy's tea…combed his hair or did any of the wee things' (1) – even then Cassie's father constantly expected her to do things for him (1)
- 'wasn't fit to do for himself' (1) – needy, incapable of looking after himself (1)
- 'So it must have been me…' (1) – created feelings of guilt in Cassie (1)

Question 1 (b)

 To get maximum marks for these 4-mark questions, your answers need to be 'very detailed'. To make sure you have written enough for the marks you should always choose three quotes and discuss each of them.

At least two of:

- 'There's been…and men…' (1) – suggests there have been several (1)
- 'pull them out of a sea of whisky' (1) – had to rescue, men as needy (1)
- 'the kiss of life' (1) – men needed Cassie to 'save' them, relied on her (1)
- 'Lying hounds' (1) – angry, disappointed, let down by men, bitter (1)
- 'every one' (1) – thinks all men are the same (1)

Question 2 (a)

 Do not worry about writing in full, grammatical sentences for questions like this. It is far more important that you comment in detail. This may mean adding ideas that occur to you in note form.

One of:

- fascinating, captivating (1) – 'All men you'd look at twice one way or another' (1)
- Not really close (1) – 'didn't really go around together' (1)
- Abused alcohol (1) – 'too drunk…drinking some more…drunk enough' (1)
- Fun-loving/selfish/Cassie recognises that they were only concerned with their own happiness (1) – 'Sure it was a party they had' (1)

Question 2 (b)

Any combination of at least two bullets about two of the men:

Michael

- Reliable (1) – 'strong feel' (1)
- Charismatic (1) – 'felt it in the back of your neck…' (1)
- Poor at expressing affection (1) – 'Sometimes he even did that' (1)

Davey

- Initially immature (1) – 'that wee boy'
- Aged by experience (1) – 'they've put age in his eyes' (1)

Martin

- Intimidating (1) – 'you'd cross the street' / 'a glower on his face like two fists hitting a table' (1)

Joe

- Cheerful (1) – 'always laughing'/'always where the crack is' (1)

Question 3

You might refer to some of the following in your answer. However, there are other possibilities that you could discuss.

- Men are never seen on stage in the play but still exert a huge influence on the female characters.

- The men are often idealised but ultimately only offer a temporary, misleading escape. Cassie describes Michael as 'just a bit of excitement'.

- Several of the men are imprisoned in 'the Kesh' but are also trapped in the role that is expected of them: 'They don't want to be raging and screaming and hurting…'

- The women in the play are similarly trapped in assigned roles: 'Spoil the wee girls with housework and reproaches'

- The characters are often seen performing domestic tasks and Deirdre's destruction of Nora's fabric seems to be an assault on the gender roles expected of women

- However, at the end Marie seems to find comfort in her motherly role, making breakfast and ending the play with the words, 'I'll put the kettle on'

Drama, Text 2: *Tally's Blood* by Anne-Marie di Mambro

Question 4

 HINT There have been tensions throughout the play between Massimo and Rosinella. This is the point where they come to a head and is a major turning point in the play. While revising the play, you should make sure that you identify key scenes, such as the opening, turning point/s and climax.

At least four of:

- Rosinella ignores Massimo's attempts to discuss Hughie (1)

- Rosinella wants to return to Italy (1)

- Massimo needs to consider their business (1)

- Massimo is upset that Rosinella never agreed to go with him before (1)

- Massimo accuses Rosinella of selfishness (1) and of feeling sorry for herself (1)

- Massimo leaves (1)

- Rosinella is devastated (1)

Question 5

 HINT The question asks about 'emotions'. Make sure you include in your answer adjectives that describe feelings.

Emotions – initially desolate, desperate but determined (1), then shocked and devastated (1)

AND one of:

- Use of commands, e.g. 'Take me' (1) – desperate (1)
- Short sentences (1) – abrupt, decisive, determined (1)
- Words suggesting she has given up on Scotland (1) – 'I can't face it', 'I don't care'... (1)
- Repetition of 'just' (1) – decisive, clear in thinking (1)
- 'If you knew...' (1) – indignant, offended (1)
- 'Massimo...please' (1) – pleading (1)
- *'Rosinella shattered'* (1) – devastated (1)

Question 6

> *HINT* There are various techniques used here: questions, block capitals, repetition. Make sure you are familiar with the way that a variety of techniques can be used by the playwright.

Two of:

- Series of questions (1) – he is thinking of practicalities, disbelief (1)
- 'YOU'RE...YOU...YOU', use of block capitals (1) – raised voice, emphasising her selfishness (1)
- 'To hell...to hell...' (1) – accusatory, believes Rosinella is uncaring (1)
- 'wish to God...God knows' (1) – cursing (1)
- 'did you ever...' (1) – feels Rosinella is inconsiderate (1)
- *'Voice breaks'* (1) – overcome by emotion (1)

Question 7

You might refer to some of the following in your answer. However, there are other possibilities that you could discuss.

- Rosinella is a conflicting character: she is very caring but also extremely selfish. She is deeply prejudiced against her adopted country but regularly refuses to return to Italy with Massimo. She loves Lucia but smothers her.
- Near the beginning of the play we see Rosinella vigorously defending her right to look after Lucia, establishing her love.
- However, she also shows her bigotry:

  — Rosinella is hostile towards Bridget.

  — Rosinella is cruel to Hughie, refusing to see him as a worthy suitor for Lucia and showing no appreciation for the work he does, even though he works 'like a Trojan'.

- However, she finally realises the error of her ways and works to make sure Lucia and Hughie get together. She seems to rediscover an understanding of the power of romantic love, which initially made her elope with Massimo

Drama, Text 3: *Sailmaker* by Alan Spence

Question 8

At least two of:

Alec

- Woken up thinking about it/disturbs his sleep (1)
- Emotions are divided (1)
- Upset (1)
- Impassive/shock (1)
- Feeling of distance (1)

Davie

AND at least two of:

- Tries to keep busy (1)
- Tries to look after Alec (1)
- Feels despair (1)

Question 9

> *HINT* You must show an understanding of what makes an 'effective opening' here. You may focus on introducing character, the relationship between Alec and Davie or the build-up of tension.

Two of:

- Use of 'it', 'the feeling' (1) – unspecified event with great significance for Alec (1)
- 'Batter. Batter.' (1) – repetition and onomatopoeia help to recreate the shock of this moment (1)
- 'Yer mammy's dead' (1) – revelation is delayed (1)
- 'Yer mammy's dead' repeated (1), showing significance of this and also the way that Davie seems to be finding it difficult to come to terms with the reality of his situation (1)
- 'real big deep sobs … my puny grief' (1) – Alec's despair (1)

Question 10 (a)

> *HINT* For 2 marks you should really try to provide two separate quotes with comments.

Davie

At least one of:

- 'There's just you an me now son' (1) – keen to look after his son (1), reveals his loneliness (1)
- 'We'll have tae make the best of it' (1) – attempts to stay positive (1)
- 'Ah'll make a cuppa tea'/'We better get this place tied up a bit son' (1) – tries to provide for son/take on role of mother, looking after the house, cooking etc. (1)

- 'As long as ye keep movin it doesnae hit ye' (1) – tries to stay busy (1)
- 'Sometimes for whole minutes ye can nearly forget about it' (1) – dark humour, relief is only temporary (1)
  - 'ye wonder for a minute where she's got tae' (1) – cannot come to terms with reality of situation (1)
  - 'Christ this is it this is me for the rest ae ma days' (1) – despair (1)

Question 10 (b)

At least one of:

Alec

- 'Everything was the same' (1) – finds it strange that the rest of the world seems unaffected (1)
- 'I don't know what I had expected. Jesus to come walking…' (1) – questions his faith (1)
- 'something from a dream' (1) – does not feel real (1)
- 'My mother was dead' repeated (1) – trying to come to terms, cannot escape from the knowledge (1)
- 'a wee patch of clear blue' (1) – temporary relief (1)

Question 11

You might refer to some of the following in your answer. However, there are other possibilities that you could discuss.

- A good starting point would be to look at the way that Alec continues to be haunted by the memory of his mother's death.
- Alec grows up during the play.
- The technique employed here, where lighting and stage directions allow Alec to speak directly to the audience, is used elsewhere in the play; these monologues provide insights into Alec's thoughts and state of mind.
- At points Alec becomes very disillusioned.
- Alec seeks comfort in religion but later rejects it.
- He seems to want to break free of his circumstances but is held back by financial problems and his loyalty to his father.

Prose, Text 1: *The Telegram* by Iain Crichton Smith

Question 12

 HINT The question asks about **differences**. Your answer needs to make clear the contrast between the two women.

Any four of:

- One is slim, the other overweight (1)
- The thin woman's son is an officer, the fat woman's a sailor (1)
- The thin woman's son had studied at university, the other left school at a young age (1)

- The thin woman came from another village originally, the fat woman has always lived there (1)

- The thin woman wanted to improve her (and her son's) social standing, by implication the fat woman did not (1)

Question 13

 Make sure that your chosen quotation, and the comments you make on it, focus on the way **tension** is created. The tension is shown in the relationship between the two women and also the writer's description of Macleod and the letter he brings.

One of:

- 'black clothes' (1) – connotations of death and sadness (1)

- 'the yellow was both strange and unnatural' (1) – incongruity, brings fear as terror of war in the outside world intrudes on the village (1)

- 'It's Macleod again' (1) – his arrival seems regular, almost expected, death has become familiar (1)

- 'they spoke feverishly' (1) – trying to block out fear (1)

- 'whatever plague he was bringing' (1) – widespread disaster arrives (1)

- 'Don't worry' (1) – (failed) attempt to reassure (1)

- 'You don't know…you don't know' (1) – repetitions suggest panic (1)

- 'added without thinking' (1) – thoughtless comment as the women turn on each other (1)

Question 14

 Your answer must include **two** points: the feeling of the character and evidence to support this.

One of:

- 'thinking that the fat woman was very stupid' (1) – contemptuous (1)

- 'most of them were' (1) – bitter about not being allowed to fit in (1)

- 'they were large, fat and lazy' (1) – angry about the ignorance of the other villager, regretful about her decision to send her own son to university (1)

Question 15

Two of:

- 'sacrifices' (1) – loss, cost to mother (1)

- 'one thought of one's own family first' (1) – worry over son, feeling guilt that she hopes another family has lost a son (1)

- 'The teacher told me. I had no thought of sending him' (1) – seems to feel as if she was pressured into sending son to university (1)

- 'ten shillings' (1) – financial cost (1)

- 'When did you see me…?' (1) – wants other woman to recognise the sacrifice she made (1)

- 'marry an English girl and where will I be?' (1) – feels like she is losing her son (1)
- 'I'm sure she smokes and drinks' (1) – disapproval of young people's lifestyle (1)
- 'And he might not give me anything' (1) – debt that can never be repaid (1)
- 'He never sends me anything' (1) – lack of support (fat woman) (1)
- 'he can't go against his nature' (1) – possibly a tone of regret (1)

Question 16

You might refer to some of the following in your answer. However, there are other possibilities that you could discuss.

- *In Church* and *The Crater* also deal with the trauma of war but the other two stories focus on the combatants while this story examines the effect on the home front.
- The bond between mother and son is also explored in the story *Mother and Son*.
- The village setting, where everyone knows everyone else, is similar in *The Painter* and *The Red Door*.
- The hostility between the two women in this story is, for the most part, suppressed. In the story *The Painter* the antagonism explodes into cruelty and violence.

Prose, Text 2: *Zimmerobics* by Anne Donovan

Question 17

> *HINT* In an extract which is written in first person narrative 'what happens' can be as much about the thoughts, feelings and attitudes of the narrator.

Any four:

- Cheryl tells Miss Knight about the class (1)
- Miss Knight decides that she will go (1)
- Miss Knight feels out of place because she is not appropriately dressed for the class (1)
- Miss Knight enjoys the class (particularly the YMCA) (1)
- The class makes Miss Knight feel better (1)

Question 18

> *HINT* This answer will need to come from direct speech: the words that Cheryl says to Miss Knight. Try to picture her and imagine her mood or attitude as she speaks.

One of:

- 'There's lots of old folks' homes looking for something like this' (1) – knowledgeable (1)
- 'all up and down the country…Zimmerobics with Cheryl' (1) – ambitious (1)
- 'So I'll see you on Thursday then?' (1) – keen, persuasive, assertive (1)

Question 19

 Miss Knight has a strong narrative voice – try to imagine the way that she speaks and what this tells us about her character.

One of:

- 'I'll think about it' (1) – non-committal, cautious, evasive (1)

- 'I kept thinking about it' (1) – intrigued, tempted (1)

- 'impossibly shaped women…' (1) – intimidated (1)

- 'humph-backit…swollen feet' (1) – unsuited to aerobics, put off by physical limitations (1)

- 'surprised to see some of them wearing tracksuits' (1) – awkward, timid (1)

- 'like starting school and discovering that the others were wearing school uniform and you weren't' (1) – apprehensive, feels like she does not belong (1)

Question 20

 This question asks about a large section of the text. It may be helpful to look at quite separate stages – the start of the class; near the end; later in the day – to make sure you write about two quite distinct stages in her 'growing enthusiasm'.

Two of:

- 'so far so good' (1) – growing in confidence, pleased about how she has coped so far (1)

- 'we marched…raised…paused…kicked' (1) – series of verbs conveying increasing sense of rhythm and involvement (1)

- 'It was brilliant.' (1) – short statement, enthusiastic outburst (1)

- 'My body was old and decrepit, but it still worked.' (1) – sense of triumph over physical difficulty (1)

- 'I looked around and saw their faces' (1) – sense of belonging (1)

- 'as though someone had oiled all the creaky old joints' (1) – greater freedom of movement, stiffness is eased (1)

- 'a pleasant ache, an ache of life' (1) – rediscovery of fun, feels alive (1)

Question 21

You might refer to some of the following in your answer. However, there are other possibilities that you could discuss.

- Several of Donovan's stories deal with family relationships and the difficulty of communication between generations. In this story the focus is on an elderly woman who sees things differently to her niece, Catherine.

- Cross-generational relationships are explored in *Dear Santa*, *All That Glisters* and *Away in a Manger*.

- The use of first person narrative could be compared and contrasted to the first person narrative voice used in *All That Glisters* and *Away in a Manger*. Interestingly, *Zimmerobics* uses Standard English as opposed to the Scots of some other stories.

- Miss Knight's description of the 'pleasant ache' recalls the narrator of *A Chitterin Bite* who says that of jumping into the swimming pool: 'Ah hate jumpin intae the baths but ah love it as well'.
- Miss Knight's fascination with her aerobics class has another parallel in how Clare becomes enthralled with the glitter pens in *All That Glisters*.

Prose, Text 3: *The Testament of Gideon Mack* by James Robertson

Question 22

Two of:

- He is heartless (1)
- He is deceitful (1)
- His character was influenced strongly by his father (1)
- Love does not come naturally to him (1)
- As he got older he became sceptical (1)
- He no longer worries about people's opinion of him (1)

Question 23

Two of:

- 'cold' / 'ice' (1) – unfeeling (1)
- 'imagine joy, sorrow, anger' (1) – incapable of strong emotion (1)
- 'disguised' (1) – putting on an act, pretending to be like the other children (1)
- 'dutiful' (1) – did what was expected of him, behaved (1)
- 'in the shadow' (1) – felt intimidated, eclipsed by his father, unable to truly be himself (1)
- 'love is not in us' (1) – did not feel any affection (1)

Question 24

At least two of:

- 'this fire was burning deep inside' (1) – hidden passions (1)
- 'battened down, the door of the furnace tightly shut' (1) – suppressed emotions, forced to keep true emotions inside (1)
- 'like the child in the cinema whose chief anticipation lies not in the film but in wondering what he will do after it is over' (1) – unable to savour the moment and enjoy life (1)
- 'shadows…shadows' (1) – time of darkness/the unknown (1)
- 'prophet' (1) – arrogance, self-importance (1)
- 'vomited' (1) – self-loathing/disgust (1)
- 'Jonah…God…Devil' (1) – biblical references show its strong influence on his beliefs and imagination (1)
- 'madness' (1) – questioning of own sanity/linked to religion (1)

Question 25

One of:

- 'nothing was the same again' (1) – creates anticipation of a complete change (1)

- 'This is my testimony.' (1) – short sentence, suggesting giving evidence, we will find out the truth (1)

- 'Read it and believe it, or believe it not' (1) – command (1)

- '…one day soon…' (1) – anticipation of revelations (1)

Question 26

- The Christianity preached by Gideon's father is restricting, for example preventing him from watching television on a Sunday. It is a religion that is ruled by fear rather than mercy or imagination.

- Gideon rebels against this, for example telling his classmates that at university he questions his beliefs.

- However, religion offers Gideon a stable career.

- His friend, Catherine Craigie, is an atheist and Gideon enjoys her company. Indeed he uses her funeral to make his rejection of Christianity public. The description of the funeral shows the differing reactions to this: children fly kites and enjoy the sweets, while the Kirk elders disapprove.

- Gideon's discovery of the standing stone links him to pre-Christian, pagan beliefs.

- Gideon does find belief – in the Devil – after his experience in the Black Jaws, but his vision of the Devil is quite different to the conventional Satan of Christianity.

Prose, Text 4: *Kidnapped* by Robert Louis Stevenson

Question 27

At least three of:

- Alan Breck and David Balfour continue to journey through the Highlands (1).

- They come to a rocky waterfall (1).

- Alan crosses the river, jumping and using an overhanging branch to swing across (1).

- David attempts to cross in the same manner and slips (1).

- Alan catches him and saves him (1).

- They continue their journey (1).

- They come to rest on top of two large rocks which provides them with a hiding place (1).

Question 28

> *HINT*   As part of your study of the novel, it would be useful to chart the way that tension builds at various points. You might do this in writing or you could do this visually, by plotting the rising and falling tension on a graph.

Mood/atmosphere: anxiety, tension (1)

Writer's use of language (any one of):

- 'this horrible place' (1) – David is disheartened (1)

- 'dinning upon all sides' (1) – noise adds to confusion and fear (1)

- 'roaring of the falls' (1) – onomatopoeia emphasises the deafening sound (1)
- 'the water raging by' (1) – personification making the river seem angry and ruthless (1)
- 'shuddered' (1) – exhaustion, cold and terror (1)

Question 29

> **HINT** Stevenson skilfully creates climax through sentence structure. Look at the way that both Breck and Balfour's safe landings are delayed to the end of the paragraphs.

Two of:

- 'Hang or drown!' (1) – exclamation, expressing Breck's bravery and boldness (1)
- 'Then, putting his hands to his mouth…and landed safe' (1) – periodic sentence, delaying the climactic phrase 'landed safe' until the end (1)
- 'flung myself forth' (1) – David hurls himself into danger (1)
- 'that kind of anger or despair' (1) – David seems desperate (1)
- 'Sure enough…dragged me into safety' (1) – long sentence, delaying the climax of David being caught and saved (1)
- 'slipped, caught again, slipped again' (1) – each slight loss of grip described adding to tension (1)
- 'sliddering' (1) – onomatopoeic word, suggesting uncontrolled slip into the river (1)
- 'with a great strain dragged me into safety' (1) – physical effort (1)

Question 30

> **HINT** You need to make clear the contrast between Alan's emotions here and what has gone before.

- Alan seems happy, pleased with something (1). Yet they have come close to death (1)/Alan seems afraid, 'he was in mortal fear' (1)/their surroundings still seem remote and forbidding: 'bestrewd with rocks…nowhere the smoke of a house' (1).

Question 31

You might refer to some of the following in your answer. However, there are other possibilities that you could discuss.

- Stevenson includes a huge amount of detail in his description of the places where David's adventures take place, bringing factual accuracy and increased plausibility to the novel.
- Balfour is a lowlander and he is an outsider in the Highlands. In his narration, he often depicts the Highlands as barren and harsh, in the chapter 'The Flight in the Heather' for example, he bemoans 'the gloom of the weather and the country'.
- Stevenson uses setting to provide dangers and adventures that David must endure, but they also have symbolic significance, e.g. in the chapter 'The Islet' David says he is 'in a place so desert-like and lonesome' when he feels isolated and far from home.
- The House of Shaws, sitting amongst idyllic countryside, is 'a kind of ruin,' which suits the moral deprivation of David's uncle.
- David's travels throughout Scotland allow Stevenson to explore the political tensions of the time.

Prose, Text 5: *The Cone–Gatherers* **by Robin Jenkins**

Question 32

 This extract is from the very beginning of the novel, where Jenkins is establishing the setting. Remember that setting should include details of time, sounds and atmosphere as well as just place.

At least four of:

- It is in a forest of fir trees (1).

- They are near the sea (1).

- Nearby there is a large manor house (1).

- The sun is setting (1).

- It is quiet (1).

- The night is clear and stars can be seen (1).

- The noises of creatures can be heard – foxes, owls (1).

Question 33

 You might have a clear idea of the mood or atmosphere from your first reading or it may come as you begin to look for and analyse quotes. However, to make sure you get full marks make sure that you clearly state what the mood or atmosphere is.

Two of:

- 'homely' (1) – welcoming, peaceful (1)

- 'as comfortable as chairs' (1) – simile making it seem pleasant (1)

- 'Seals that had been playing tag…like children' (1) – personification, seals seem childish, innocent, creates sense of intimacy between Neil and Calum (1)

- 'A destroyer' (1) – conflict, threat of war (1)

- 'pluck the sweet resinous cores' (1) – plenty, fruitful, comfort of nature (1)

- 'chaffinches fluttered…alight' (1) – gentle, communing with nature, brothers feel that they belong (1)

- '"Careful". It was the only word…' (1) – quiet, care for brother, mood of peace and love between brothers (1)

- 'dusk like a breathing' (1) – gentle, calm mood (1)

- 'mottled yellow…bronze of beech, saffron of birches' (1) – colour, precious wealth of nature where brothers feel at home and comfortable (1)

Question 34 (a)

 Although your answer must focus on specific quotes that you have chosen from the extract, you should think about your wider knowledge of the text and its characters when answering questions like this.

Neil (one of):

- 'gazed at the great house…bitter' (1) – angry about class barriers (1)
- 'Carefu' (1) – worries about brother (1)
- 'sat motionless and silent' (1) – reflective (1)

Question 34 (b)

Calum (one of):

- 'indigenous as squirrel or bird' (1) – content in nature (1)
- 'speckled with orange needles' (1) – belongs (1)
- 'stroked the petals…gentle hands' (1) – empathetic (1)
- 'part-bird then, part-man' (1) – so much a part of nature that he is like one of the creatures (1)
- 'the terrifying mystery' (1) – struggles to understand ways (especially cruelty) of men (1)

Question 35

You might refer to some of the following in your answer. However, there are other possibilities that you could discuss.

- Jenkins often uses language and imagery of nature, e.g. when describing Duror's growing hatred: 'as if that tree of hatred and revulsion was being tossed by a gale'.
- Calum is depicted throughout the novel as empathetic towards nature, particularly when he runs to the deer which is wounded during the hunt.
- Duror has a conflicting attitude to nature, describing his hut in the woods as his 'stronghold'.
- But shows his cruelty when drowning cats and whipping dogs.
- Neil is afraid of the wood.
- Roderick sees the wood as a magical place, fantasising about *The Pilgrim's Progress* and the quest for the Holy Grail.
- Nature is in conflict, with descriptions of creatures hunting. This reflects the war being fought in the world beyond the forest. However, Jenkins also depicts the beauty of nature.

Poetry, Text 1: *War Photographer* by Carol Ann Duffy

Question 36

> *HINT*   It might be useful when revising this poem, or others which are not split into stanzas, to divide the poem into sections. Think about how the ideas progress as the poem goes on; give each section a subtitle; look at how change is marked in the poem.

Two of:

- Solitary nature of work (1), 'finally alone' (1)
- Fact he captures people at times of anguish (1), 'spools of suffering' (1)

- Dedication to work (1), 'as though…to intone a mass' (1)

- Importance of message he is trying to communicate (1), 'intone a mass' (1)

- Professionalism (1), 'He has a job to do' (1)

Question 37

Two of:

- Cold, professional approach while taking photos (1) – 'hands which did not tremble then' (1)

- Contrast of return to the commonplace (1) – 'ordinary pain…simple weather' (1)

- Trauma (1) – 'A stranger's features faintly start to twist' (1)

- Memories carried with him (1) – 'He remembers the cries…' (1)

- Drive/obligation to take pictures (1) – 'to do what someone must' (1)

Question 38

> This conclusion is different in some ways as Duffy introduces new ideas in these final lines, shifting the focus first to the editor and then the reader. However, this serves to broaden the ideas of the poem and to ask how we may respond to the images described. The final two lines focus, again, on the photographer.

Two of:

- 'a hundred agonies' (1) – links back to the idea of 'suffering' (1)

- 'his editor will pick out five or six…' (1) – professional, detached nature of editor/desire to sell newspapers, link to photographers own attitude (1)

- 'eyeballs prick with tears' (1) – emotional reaction similar to photographer's trembling hands (1)

- 'between the bath and pre-lunch beers' (1) – readers forget the images and move on in a similar way to the photographer going home (1)

- 'stares impassively'/'they do not care' (1) – again shows a lack of empathy (1)

Question 39

You might refer to some of the following in your answer. However, there are other possibilities that you could discuss.

- Like *Anne Hathaway*, the poem is concerned with the creative process.

- In contrast to *Mrs Midas* and *Havisham* the poem is told in the third person, providing a distance between reader and subject which may link to the poem's ideas.

- The memories that seem to haunt the photographer – 'the cries' – mirror the way in *Havisham* the persona remembers her betrayal every day.

- *Originally* also deals with changing emotions – in *War Photographer* the photographer's emotions change when he returns home from assignment, in *Originally* the persona experiences a more permanent change of country.

Poetry, Text 2: *Lucozade* **by Jackie Kay**

Question 40 (a)

> **HINT**   This poem is concerned with two characters: the persona and her mother. Make sure you think about the character of the mother **and** the conflicting feelings of her daughter.

Two of:

- The persona's mother is ill (1)
- The persona is concerned about her mother (1)
- The persona's mother is very strong-willed (1)
- The persona fears that her mother's condition is fatal (1)
- The persona's mother does not want the traditional gifts brought to patients in hospital (1)
- The persona's mother does not trust the doctors (1)
- The persona's mother is obese (1)

Question 40 (b)

> **HINT**   Set out your answers clearly. Make sure it is clear to the marker that you have two separate quotes and detailed comments on each. Bullet points can help.

Two of:

- 'on a high bed' (1) – hospitalised (1)
- 'sad chrysanthemums' (1) – suggest the depression of the mother (1)
- 'I am scared' (1) – concerns of persona (1)
- 'Don't bring Lucozade' (1) – imperative sentence, order, commanding character (1)
- 'fades' (1) – weakness (1)
- 'a blur, a swarm' (1) – confusion (1)
- 'doctors with their white lies' (1) – mistrust (1)
- 'Did you think…?' (1) – ungrateful (1)
- 'too much about size' (1) – concern about weight (1)

Question 41

Two of:

- 'What I want to know' (1) – taking charge (1)
- 'the big brandy…the dirty big meringue' (1) – list of pleasures, alcohol, cakes… (1)
- 'big brandy, the generous gin' (1) – alliteration, seems to be savouring the idea of these luxuries (1)
- 'I am sixteen' (1) – young, ill-prepared for dealing with her mother's mortality (1)
- 'Tell your father' (1) – imperative, commanding, asserting control (1)
- 'Grapes have no imagination' (1) – disdain (1)

Question 42

 HINT You must give an understanding of what a conclusion should do. You might refer to summarising ideas or, in this instance, a change of mood.

One of:

- 'My mother' (1) – possessive, proud (1)
- 'light' (1) – contrast with concerns about weight (1)
- 'radiant' (1) – light and cheerful (1)
- 'She is beautiful' (1) – short statement, affection for mother (1)
- 'I carry the orange nostalgia' (1) – happy memories (1)
- 'singing' (1) – happy (1)

Question 43

You might refer to some of the following in your answer. However, there are other possibilities that you could discuss.

- All of the poems by Jackie Kay in the selection deal with family relationships.
- The poem *Divorce* is told from the point of view of the daughter, comically rejecting her parents.
- *My Grandmother's Houses* depicts another strong female character who rejects her new house initially, as the mother in this poem rejects her gifts.
- *Gap Year* is told from the point of view of a mother who feels she is losing her daughter.
- Strong concrete symbols feature in various poems: Lucozade and chrysanthemums in this poem, orchids in *Keeping Orchids* and 'The sideboard solid as a coffin' in *My Grandmother's Houses*.

Poetry, Text 3: *Assisi* by Norman MacCaig

Question 44

 HINT Careful reading of this question shows that a successful answer will deal with dwarf, priest and tourists separately.

- Dwarf – begging, sitting outside church (1)
- Priest – talking about the churches and their artwork (1)
- Tourists – chatting, following the priest (1)

Question 45

Two of:

- 'slumped like a half-filled sack' (1) – simile, seems inanimate, incomplete, object of pity (1)
- 'tiny twisted legs' (1) – misshapen, painful (1)
- 'from which sawdust might run' (1) – objectifies the dwarf, dwarf is dehumanised (1)
- 'three tiers of churches' (1) – magnificence of church contrasts with the beggar's infirmity (1)

- 'St Francis, brother of the poor, talker with birds' (1) – contrast of magnificent church with pitiful dwarf (1)
- 'over whom he had the advantage of not being dead yet' (1) – ironic tone, expressing disgust at disregard for the dwarf, injustice and inequality (1)

Question 46

 HINT The word 'developing' here is important. You should try to link the ideas expressed in these lines with ideas that either link back to the first stanza, or forward to the final stanza.

Two of:

- Scene shifts to inside the church, dwarf is excluded (1)
- Priest does not care for the dwarf, too busy acting as a tour guide (1)
- Frescoes are not helping poor, they are attracting tourists and providing financial gain for the church (1)
- Ironic tone of 'clever…cleverness' – disapproval of the priest (1)

Question 47

Tourists

Emotional response – disgust, distaste, disapproval (1)

AND one of:

- 'rush of tourists' (1) – tourists are in a hurry, refusing to take note of either dwarf or the frescoes, not learning the lessons of St Francis (1)
- 'clucking contentedly, fluttered' (1) – imagery comparing tourists to birds, they lack intelligence or consideration (1)
- 'as he scattered the grain of the Word' (1) – biblical reference making clear that the words and lessons of the Bible have been corrupted (1)
- 'It was they who had passed' (1) – tourists ignored the plight of the beggar (1)

OR

Beggar

Emotional response – pity, sympathy (1)

AND one of:

- 'ruined temple' (1) – focus returns to the dwarf, compares him to something destroyed, yet sacred (1)
- 'whose eyes wept pus, whose back was higher than his head, whose lopsided mouth…' (1) – shocking description of extent of dwarf's disabilities, evokes sympathy (1)
- 'said *Grazie* in a voice as sweet as a child's' (1) – innocence, contrasts with the corruption and hypocrisy of the priest (1)
- 'a bird's when it spoke to St Francis' (1) – reference to St Francis, dwarf provides reminder of need for real Christian charity (1)

Question 48

You might refer to some of the following in your answer. However, there are other possibilities that you could discuss.

- Like *Basking Shark*, a chance encounter provokes reflection on a wider theme.

- Imagery is used to create a clear picture of a person who deserves pity in this poem. In *Visiting Hour*, MacCaig's imagery is also effective in depicting a figure who is extremely ill.

- The 'distance of pain' MacCaig describes in *Visiting Hour* between patient and visitor might make for an interesting discussion. The speaker in *Assisi* seems to want to close the distance between himself and the dwarf, while the priests and tourists seem happy to maintain that distance.

- This desire to make a connection is similar to the persona in *Aunt Julia* trying, too late, to understand his aunt.

Poetry, Text 4: *Trio* by Edwin Morgan

Question 49 (a)

> *HINT* Make sure in your revision of texts that you are clear about the main themes.

Two of:

- Importance of intimacy (1)

- Christmas, whether Christian or pagan, is a time of celebration (1)

- Power of youth and vitality (1)

- Idea of rebirth/new life (1)

- Joyful mood (1)

Question 49 (b)

> *HINT* There are a lot of possibilities here. Make sure that you choose two that you are confident about analysing in detail.

Two of:

- Balanced structure of 'the young man…the girl…the girl' (1) links the three together (1)

- Word choice of 'quickly…swells' (1) suggests they are bursting with energy (1)

- Word choice of 'three of them laughing' (1) suggests they share their happiness and delight (1)

- 'the three' (1) links to idea of Christian trinity, Three Wise Men… (1)

- Word choice of 'Christmas lights…silver tinsel…sprig of mistletoe' (1) make clear his point about the fun of Christmas (1)

- Word choice of 'cloud of happiness' (1) makes clear the jubilant mood (1)

- Exclamation of 'Wait till he sees this but!' (1) shows the excitement of the young man (1)

- Word choice of 'baby…bright eyes' (1) adds to mood of happiness and makes clear the theme of rebirth (1)

- 'mistletoe' is a pagan symbol of life (1), appropriated by Christianity (1)

Question 50

Two of:

- Series of exclamations (1) 'Orphean sprig…!' (1)

- 'Orphean' (1) – return from underworld, defeat of death (1)

- 'Melting…warm' (1) – importance of affection and kindness (1)

- Biblical reference in 'The vale of tears' (1) continues idea of Christianity (1)

- 'The vale of tears is powerless' (1) suggests that the exuberance of youth can overcome darkness (1)

- 'Whether Christ is born, or is not born' (1) suggests doubt about Christian beliefs (1)

- 'Monsters of the year go blank' (1) defeat of fear and death (1)

Question 51

> **HINT**   A **conclusion** to a poem often shows the poet or persona reflecting on the significance of the incident they are describing. Here the brief encounter with the three revellers brings a sense of joy and positivity.

One of:

- 'the three' (1) – return to idea of trinity (1)

- 'vanished (yet not vanished…)' (1) – idea that life is fleeting but still valuable (1)

- 'men and beasts, and music' (1) – baby, Chihuahua and guitar (1)

- 'laughter' (1) – joy (1)

- 'like a guard' (1) – human happiness protects against the fear/knowledge of death (1)

- 'at the end of this winter's day' (1) – winter over and spring and rebirth shall return (1)

Question 52

You might refer to some of the following in your answer. However, there are other possibilities that you could discuss

- *Winter* also uses the symbol of winter to reflect on death and the passing of time.

- *Good Friday* describes a person during a Christian festival.

- *In the Snack Bar* also looks at human nature but seems to conclude less optimistically.

- *Slate* also investigates man's transience.

WORKED ANSWERS — Practice Exam B

Critical Reading Section B: Critical Essay

DRAMA

1. It is often said that all drama depends upon conflict so this question should provide a good opportunity for writing. However, to answer the question well, there are some things that you must consider. 'Conflict' does not necessarily mean a direct argument or violence. The main character might experience internal conflict like the title character of *Othello* or Willie Loman in *Death of a Salesman*. The main character may be in conflict with another character – Othello's jealousy and insecurity is brought about by the treachery of Iago; Frank and Rita disagree over the necessity of change in *Educating Rita*. The character may also be in conflict with society like John Proctor in *The Crucible*. It is vital that you state at the beginning of your essay what the conflict is and describe throughout your essay how it is conveyed by the playwright. When dealing with a character who experiences different conflicts you should structure your essay so that you deal with each clearly.

> *HINT* Learning quotes is an important part of your revision. However, as well as the quote itself you must make sure you revise the context of the quote and how you can analyse the quote. Also, make sure that you justify your use of the quote and its significance to the central concerns your essay identifies.

2. Before you begin answering this question you should stop and consider what makes an 'effective opening'. It is essential that an opening should introduce the main characters, the setting and the source of conflict. However, an opening should also grab your attention: what makes the opening gripping or intriguing? Also, to fully answer the question you should describe how the themes or 'central concerns' are introduced. The opening scenes of *Romeo and Juliet* for example introduce the violence and rivalry which will bring about the tragic conclusion. Also, make sure that you relate the effect of the opening to specific dramatic techniques such as the sound effects, lighting and dialogue which Liz Lochead uses at the beginning of *Britannia Rules*.

PROSE

3. Character development should be one of the key areas of your study of any text. There is a lot to say about, for example Ralph's descent into savagery in *The Lord of the Flies* or the way Scout grows up in *To Kill a Mockingbird*. The potential danger here is that you have too much to say. A successful answer will give clear signposts to show stages in the development of the character. You should begin by describing how the author establishes character at the beginning. Make sure you include how the writer depicts the change in character through techniques like dialogue and symbolism.

> *HINT* It may be helpful when revising to find visual methods for revising things like character development. You could try using storyboards or charts depicting a character's rise and fall. This might provide a useful summary of what you have learned and, if nothing else, should provide a little variety in your revision.

4. This question allows many possibilities. However, you must be careful not to simply say why they are important to plot. Make sure you deal with key moments' importance in character development and illustrating theme. There are many examples of texts which would provide material for this question. For example the short story *Mary Moon and the Stars* has a clear turning point where the narrator must decide whether Mary Moon really is her friend, and the themes of friendship and growing up are skilfully conveyed by Janice Galloway. Hassan's assault in *The Kite Runner* is significant for the narrator but also has a huge emotional impact on the reader.

> *HINT* Revising key moments is vital. It will not only help with questions like question 4 here, it will also help you to focus on key moments when answering questions which address the whole text. Using phrases like 'turning point' and 'climax' will show the marker you are clear about the structure of the text as a whole.

POETRY

5. There are many poems about interesting characters, such as Crichton Smith's *You'll Take a Bath*. Often poets adopt a persona and these may be the characters that you choose to write about. The emotional impact of the model in Duffy's *Standing Female Nude* or the Duke in *My Last Duchess* is enhanced by the way that they speak directly to the reader. Our emotional response to these characters change as the poems progress and charting this change through clear topic sentences and relevant quotes would make for a successful essay. You should make clear how poetic techniques, such as the repetition in Maya Angelou's *Still I Rise* help to convey character.

> *HINT*   Evaluation is vital in all critical essays. You need to focus on what the text meant to **you**, or how it made **you** feel. Try to find time in your revision to set aside your notes and reread the text, thinking carefully about its impact.

6. One of the great subjects of poetry is depicting the natural world and man's place in the world. From the Romantic poets to contemporaries like Kathleen Jamie there are many possibilities to choose from here. Robert Burns described setting in detail but also used it as a means of exploring themes such as love and man's cruelty. However, urban settings too provide material for poets: Blake's *London* would provide an excellent topic for this essay. Notice that the question says 'setting is a significant feature'. You should make sure you relate setting to the themes the writer is interested in.

FILM and TV DRAMA

7. It should be clear from the question that you need to specify which character you are going to write about. But you also need to make clear at the start of your essay what is 'interesting' about them. Are they an admirable hero? An attractive villain? Or someone you can relate to thrust into a difficult situation? A strong answer will not just relate what the character does but show how media techniques create an emotional response in you, the viewer.

> *HINT*   To write well about film and TV drama you should have specialist knowledge about camera angles, lighting etc. But don't forget that elements like characterisation, theme and plot are just as important as they are for studying literary texts.

8. You may well be familiar with genre and you can probably recognise the genre of a film from its trailer or poster. This question requires you to show an understanding of how you know this. A structured approach is, of course, vital for any critical essay. It may be best to structure an essay such as this around several key areas: plot, character, setting, theme. . . 'Classics' of a genre, like the Western *The Searchers* or the sci-fi film *2001: A Space Odyssey* helped to define the genre conventions and provide rich pickings. Other films subvert conventions or even combine conventions of different genres.

LANGUAGE STUDY

9. After specifying which geographical area you will study you should provide examples of the differences between this variety of English and Standard English. You must make certain that you don't slip into simply listing differences as the question specifies a discussion of the advantages or disadvantages the variety has.

You will also need to show a clear understanding of the way that grammar and syntax is different, so will need to have a really clear grasp of the technical aspects of language.

10. The same stories feature in dozens of newspapers every day; the same topics are discussed in magazines; the same issues explored in documentaries. There are many possibilities to explore. You could contrast the way that a controversial story is dealt with in newspapers with different political leanings, for example *The Independent* and *The Daily Telegraph*. Documentaries taking opposing sides of the debate about global warming might also provide interesting material but you should only tackle this question if you have studied the texts in class and are clear that you can write answers with the focus on language.

Answers to Practice Exam C

WORKED ANSWERS — Practice Exam C

Reading for Understanding, Analysis and Evaluation

Question 1 (a)

Two of:

- Our personality is decided by our relatives who have been influenced by their surroundings (1).

- There is a very close connection between people and the place they are brought up (1).

- The TV show *Who Do You Think You Are?* owes its success to people's interest in our connection to our forefathers (1).

- We are happy to return home when we travel (1).

- Our personal interactions are influenced by our environment (1).

Question 1 (b)

> This article strongly expresses the writer's opinion. There are a lot of possibilities to choose from. Some – 'rooted', 'shaped' – explore similar ideas. Make sure you choose enough examples to make a range of comments.

Two of:

- 'rooted' (1) – fixed, growing from out of 'the wider community' (1)

- 'shaped' (1) – moulded, created (1)

- 'connected umbilically' (1) – like mother and child (1)

- 'double helix…DNA' (1) – link compared to genetic code which defines our personality (1)

- 'tantalising' (1) – enticing, fascinating (1)

- 'felt keenly' (1) – intensity of emotion (1)

- 'warm attachment' (1) – affection (1)

- 'never wavers' (1) – constant (1)

Question 2

> The word 'difference' here means that your answer must show an understanding of the contrast between the writer's criticism of Scottish squares and his praise of those in other countries.

- In other countries they have succeeded in creating interesting city squares/city squares express what the cities are like (1).

- In Scotland we have not achieved this/we have not created squares that are representative of their cities' personality (1).

Question 3

> **HINT** A good first stage when answering an 'in your own words' question is to identify the key words, which you may do by highlighting or underlining them. For example here you need to find an alternative for words such as 'magnet' and 'visitors'.

Two of:

- To be the living hub of the community (1)
- To attract tourists (1)
- To provide a place for people to meet regularly (1)
- To provide a scene for significant events (1)

Question 4

> **HINT** You must write about both squares. Separate out your comments about each square to make your points clear to the marker.

St Mark's

Two of:

- Provides a way of saying what has happened to its inhabitants (1)
- It is energetic (1)
- It is a hub which connects different parts of the city (1)

Times Square

Two of:

- Is somewhere where people gather and socialise (1)
- It expresses something about its city (1)
- It plays an important part in the lives of New York's inhabitants (1)

Question 5

Two of:

- 'bright' (1) – colourful and lively (1)
- 'brash' (1) – loud, proud, full of energy (1)
- 'announces loudly and proudly' (1) – personifies New York, broadcasting the character of the city (1)
- 'blaring' (1) – loud (1)
- 'buzz' (1) – constant (1)
- 'bite-sized taster' (1) – New York in miniature, giving a sense of what the whole city is like (1)

Question 6

> **HINT** This question is worth 2 marks. You need to say what the writer's attitude is and provide a quotation that supports this.

- Attitude – disdain, disappointment (1)
- Evidence – 'failed so dismally', 'stumbles, staggers and slumps', 'embarrassing' (1)

Question 7

 The writer has several suggestions. Even single words such 'eat' and 'relax' provide material for your answer, as long as you find other ways to express these ideas.

Three of:

- Make it somewhere that people want to spend time (1)
- And feel safe (1)
- Socialise (1)
- Dine (1)
- Unwind (1)
- Reflect and think (1)
- Make it a meeting place for artistic events (1)
- And business meetings (1)

Question 8

 This question is worth 3 marks. That means that you need to go into significant detail about the image and the ideas it suggests.

Detailed analysis for up to 3 marks.

- 'untangling the double helix which is our defining DNA' – compares the connection between people and place to the genetic material that defines our characteristics, shows that the link lasts a long time, is unavoidable, happens without our knowledge (3)

OR

- Times Square is 'a bite-sized taster of the city' makes reference to the 'Big Apple' name for New York, making clear that the square gives a condensed version of the entire city, suggests that the experience is sensual… (3)

OR

- 'Scotland once again stumbles, staggers and slumps' – personification makes Scotland seem like a weak person, out of control of movement, lurching without thought or consideration into mistaken decisions… (3)

Question 9

Four of:

- Our personalities are shaped by our links to where we come from (1).
- City squares around the world express this connection (1).
- In Scotland we do not have city squares to be proud of (1).
- In Scotland we have failed to plan these squares sufficiently (1).
- The writer believes that we should redesign George Square to make it better (1).

WORKED ANSWERS — Practice Exam C

Critical Reading, Section A: Scottish Text

Drama, Text 1: *Bold Girls* by Rona Munro

Question 1 (a)

Two of:

- Nowhere else to go (1)
- Her children (1)
- Her work (1)
- Her home (1)
- Memories of Michael (1)

Question 1 (b)

Two of:

- Her children are growing up (1)
- She can't afford to clothe them (1)
- Her job is dull (1)
- Her job does not pay well (1)
- She is struggling to pay the bills (1)

Question 2 (a)

> **HINT**   This extract leads up to the moment when Cassie reveals that she had an affair with Michael. The exam questions might not focus on the key moments in the plot. As well as revising these key moments, make sure you are familiar with the moments which lead up to dramatic confrontations and, indeed, their repercussions.

Marie

One of:

- 'I've a lot to be thankful for' (1) – optimistic (1)
- 'That's what's great about a Saturday night out with you Cassie' (1) – increasingly sarcastic (1)
- 'I've had better times with Michael…' (1) – grateful, loving (1)
- 'It's a warming kind of thought' (1) – affectionate, deluded (1)

Question 2 (b)

Cassie

Two of:

- 'How do you. . . How do you…' (1) – confrontational (1)
- 'I'm just wicked' (1) – self-critical (1)

- 'two wee boys…a part-time job' (1) – frustrated, pessimistic (1)
- 'That mug was me' (1) – filled with regret (1)
- 'you'll be damp in the end anyway' (1) – disillusioned (1)

Question 3

 Be careful not to repeat your answer to the previous question. There may be some overlap but it is important that you keep the focus on the key idea here: conflict.

Two of:

- Cassie's constant questions, pushing Marie more and more (1)
- Marie's growing sarcasm, such as 'you just know how to look at the bright side of things, don't you?' (1)
- Marie's implied criticism of Joe, showing that she is starting to fight back (1)
- Cassie picking up Marie's use of 'warming', and turning it round – 'you'll be damp in the end anyway' (1)
- The final line showing that Cassie is also criticising Michael, attacking the thing that Marie holds most dear/ finally preparing to reveal their affair (1)

Question 4

You might refer to some of the following in your answer. However, there are other possibilities that you could discuss.

- Cassie is described in the stage directions when she first appears as 'sceptical, sharp-tongued'.
- Throughout the play she wants to escape, even saying that she would abandon her children in doing so.
- She hides the money that she has saved behind the picture of Michael.
- Her behaviour is provocative, for example enjoying the attention of men in the club: 'What, are they looking? … Let them. '
- She accuses her mother, Nora, of favouring her brother, Martin.
- She even defends her father, saying that he only hit Nora because she provoked him: 'You should have left him alone. '
- Yet, despite her faults Cassie remains a sympathetic character.

Drama, Text 2: *Tally's Blood* by Ann Marie di Mambro

Question 5

 Notice that this question does not specify that you should look in certain lines. Therefore answers can come from anywhere in the extract.

Two of:

- 'Hughie deeply engrossed' (1) – concentrating, lost in his task (1)
- 'surveys it with satisfaction' (1) – takes pride in his work (1)
- 'Takes a bottle of ginger' (1) – feels at home, feels he deserves a reward (1)

- 'Chuffed' (1) – Hughie is pleased with himself (1)
- 'Because I work here that's how come' (1) – feels like he belongs, proud (1)

Question 6

Two of:

- 'indignant' (1) – cross, outraged (1)
- 'She goes right up to him' (1) – confrontational (1)
- 'eyeing him up and down suspiciously' (1) – she shows that she does not trust him (1)
- 'self-righteous' (1) – Lucia asserts her superiority (1)
- 'Hughie Devlin!' (1) – exclamation, suggesting her anger (1)
- Repetition of 'my Uncle Massimo's' (1) – asserting her right to the shop and its contents (1)
- 'You better not…' (1) – threat (1)

Question 7

One of:

- 'eyes the bottle' (1) – cautious, suspicious (1)
- 'wiping the top of it with the palm of her hand' (1) – makes clear that she thinks it is dirty (1)
- 'takes a dainty sip' (1) – acts as if she is very delicate (1)
- 'she tilts her head back and takes huge gulps' (1) – enjoys the drink, forgetting her inhibitions (1)

Question 8

 HINT Throughout your study of drama you should keep in mind the reaction of the **audience**. Although you will study the text in detail, try not to lose track of the fact that plays are written to be performed and to create an emotional response.

One of:

- 'If you get…' (1) – matter-of-fact tone, Hughie seems unconcerned (1)
- 'horrified scream' (1) – contrast with her enjoyment of the drink/her ladylike manner previously (1)
- 'spits out the liquid…showering Hughie' (1) – physical humour, shock and contrast to previous behaviour (1)
- A general comment about the surprising nature of the event would be awarded 1 mark

Question 9

You might refer to some of the following in your answer. However, there are other possibilities that you could discuss.

- Massimo has asked Hughie to talk to Lucia so that she speaks English.
- Lucia often treats Hughie cruelly but they become steadily closer.
- There is discomfort between them which conveys the theme of racial tension, for example when Hughie pretends to be a fighter plane and when they play 'schools'.

- They comfort each other and they mark the closeness of their relationship when they become 'ginger-sister' and 'ginger-brother'.

- In Act Two Hughie has fallen in love with Lucia.

- Rosinella thinks that he is not good enough for Lucia. She destroys his love letter.

- Hughie is too nervous to confess his love for Lucia, despite her prompting: '*Hughie's cue to say he loves her: he hovers: misses it*'.

- Hughie gives her his knife, his most precious possession, when she goes to Italy.

- Hughie follows Lucia to Italy and, helped by Rosinella, they elope.

Drama, Text 3: *Sailmaker* by Alan Spence

Question 10

One of:

- 'Imagine' (1) – they still have dreams for the future (1)

- 'Getting *paid* for it!' (1) – expanding on the dream, exclamation suggests Ian is getting caught up in his vision (1)

- '*really…paid*' (1) – italics emphasises Ian's excitement (1)

- 'better…Best…Better' (1) – superlatives (1)

- 'sailmaker…tick man' (1) – ambitions to achieve more than their fathers (1)

Question 11 (a)

> **HINT**   You may find quotations to analyse in both stage directions and dialogue.

Davie (two of):

- '*shakes head*' (1) – resigned to fate (1)

- 'Week's notice' (1) – minor sentence, abrupt and short with Billy (1)

- 'Try tellin them that!' (1) – exasperation (1)

- 'Scrubbed…Laid off. Redundant' (1) – wallowing in pity (1)

- 'Turn roon an kick ye in the teeth' (1) – sense of injustice (1)

- 'Nothin.' (1) – devoid of hope (1)

Question 11 (b)

Billy (two of):

- 'Bastards' (1) – anger (1)

- 'But that wasnae your fault!' (1) – indignant (1)

- 'Ah might be able tae…' (1) – seeking a solution, possibly due to guilt (1)

- 'Somethin better…' (1) – optimistic (1)

Question 12

> *HINT*   Make clear what is **different** and back up your answer with evidence.

- Alec tries to seem more optimistic/pleased to escape from a job he didn't enjoy (1)
- 'Better than nothing'/'Ach that was a lousy job anyway' (1)

Question 13

You might refer to some of the following in your answer. However, there are other possibilities that you could discuss.

- Ian and Alec are close at the beginning of the play, playing and sharing comics.
- However, Ian seems much more mature, whereas Alec is a dreamer.
- For example, when Alec talks proudly about the rhyme his father made up, Ian exclaims: 'Your da didnae write that!'
- And Ian teases Alec regularly: 'Daftie!'
- There is comedy in their early scenes together, sharing comics, playing football and imagining being cannibals.
- However, when Alec takes more interest in religion, Ian's mockery betrays greater tension.
- And they take very different paths: Ian gaining a scholarship and studying Latin, which Alec seems to resent.
- However, it is Ian who escapes the limits of his upbringing, moving to Aberdeen and 'Doin all right'.
- Whereas Alec remains in poverty, held back by his father.

Prose, Text 1: *The Painter* by Iain Crichton Smith

Question 14

- He believes that Roderick will use it to cut/harvest a crop (1)
- But he uses it to threaten his father-in-law (1)

Question 15

Two of:

- 'At first I thought…but this was not at all…' (1) – growing realisation of what Roderick intends to do (1)
- 'There was, apart from his voice, a great silence…' (1) – Roderick's voice is the only noise against a tense, quiet background (1)
- 'something really frightening and irresponsible' (1) – vagueness of 'something', creates anticipation (1)
- 'as if all the poison' (1) – deadly, destructive (1)
- 'seethed around' (1) – intense emotions, boiling and churning inside Roderick (1)
- 'the madness which was shattering the silence' (1) – lack of reason, anything could happen (1)
- 'Then they began to fight.' (1) – short, abrupt sentence, climax (1)

Question 16

One of:

- 'the others, excited and horrified' (1) – other inhabitants of the village feel a mixture of enthusiasm and terror (1)

- 'sitting comfortably' (1) – the painter is at ease (1)

- 'no expression on his face' (1) – seems to feel no emotion (1)

- 'cold clear intensity' (1) – fixed entirely on his art (1)

- 'nor any time did he make any attempt to pull his chair back' (1) – shows no fear (1)

Question 17

 HINT   This paragraph mixes description of the painter ('He turned on me such a gaze of blind fury') and the narrator. Make sure you only select details which refer to the narrator.

Two of:

- 'seethed through me' (1) – the same word used about Roderick, the narrator feels equally enraged and aggressive (1)

- 'most bitter disgust' (1) – the narrator is horrified (1)

- 'You may think I was wrong' (1) – expects moral judgement (1)

- 'deliberately' (1) – careful, planned (1)

- 'I would have beaten him' (1) – intends to cause pain (1)

- 'I tore the painting into small pieces and scattered them' (1) – wants to completely obliterate the painting (1)

- 'fury and disgust' (1) – narrator does not think about the village, is only motivated by anger (1)

Question 18

You might refer to some of the following in your answer. However, there are other possibilities that you could discuss.

- This story depicts village relationships exploding into violence.

- Violence is depicted as similarly horrifying in the stories which focus on war: *The Crater* and *In Church*. The latter story, in particular, depicts characters who have completely lost sight of any moral or spiritual guidance.

- The tensions of village life are also portrayed in *The Telegram*. Like the painter in this story, the thin woman is still regarded as an outsider.

- The psychological cruelty of *Mother and Son* grinds down the main character, John.

- While Roderick and the narrator break free of their inhibitions violently, the narrator of *The Red Door* does so in search of love, gaining 'pride and spirit' from his brightly painted door.

Prose, Text 2: *A Chitterin Bite* by Anne Donovan

Question 19 (a)

 HINT   This story, and this extract, moves between Mary as a child and Mary as an adult.

At least two of:

- Mary storms away (1)

- Agnes convinces her to go to the cinema (1)

- They go on the double-date (1)

- Mary is unhappy with her date (1)

Question 19 (b)

 HINT   It is easy to get caught up in just writing about the word choice. You will get a mark for quoting but your answer must make clear how the language of the story expresses Mary's **feelings**.

Two of:

- 'every week…scrambling…sharing…(1) – description of the comforting, enjoyable routine of going to the cinema with Agnes (1)

- 'What?' (1) – surprise (1)

- 'unlinked ma airm' (1) – wants to protest, show change in relationship (1)

- 'marched on, starin ahead' (1) – sulking, feeling of rejection (1)

- 'you don't need me tae come too' (1) – Mary feels surplus to requirements (1)

- 'dirty-fair hair' (1) – critical of Jimmy (1)

- 'wee skinny laddie…red lips like a lassie', 'the sourness of the aftershave he must of plastered on his baby cheeks' (1) – disappointed with Shuggie (1)

- 'the airm rest forms a barrier between me and her' (1) – feels separated from Agnes, there is an obstacle in the way of their friendship (1)

Question 20 (a)

HINT   When revising this story look carefully at the similarities and differences between Mary as a child and Mary as a woman.

At least two of:

- Mary is phoned by the man she is having an affair with, Matthew (1)

- They arrange a meeting at lunchtime (1)

- Matthew confronts Mary about giving him a love-bite (1)

Question 20 (b)

One of:

- 'I don't expect…' (1) – surprise (1)

- 'Not so soon…not at work, not at ten o'clock' (1) – repetition of 'not' emphasising the unexpected nature of the call (1)

- 'bright shiny…bright shiny perfectly modulated' (1) – in control (1)

- *'Make it quarter to…'* (1) – reasserting control (1)

- 'I notice a few stray bristly hairs' (1) – begins to get sense that something is not quite right (1)

- *'Maybe a night of passion…'* (1) – flirtatious, happy (1)

- 'I look him straight in the eyes' (1) – defiant (1)

Question 20 (c)

One of:

- *'What?'* (1) – abrupt, communication seems forced and uncertain between them (1)

- *'Speaking of bites…'* (1) – sudden change of tone, ellipsis suggesting that there is more left unsaid (1)

- 'tight into a fist' (1) – pent up anger, frustration (1)

Question 21

You might refer to some of the following in your answer. However, there are other possibilities that you could discuss.

- In several stories – *Away in a Manger, Dear Santa, Zimmerobics* – Donovan addresses gaps between the generations.

- In this story, Donovan looks at the same character as a child and an adult, exploring the loss of innocence, whereas in *Away in a Manger* for example, the child's innocence contrasts with her mother.

- The use of Scots by Mary as a child connects her to children from the other stories.

- The story *Virtual Pals* also alternates between a Scots register and Standard English, this time for comic effect.

- Like the narrator of *Dear Santa* Mary craves affection.

- And like the narrator of *All That Glisters* Mary acts impulsively to show her love.

Prose, Text 3: *The Testament of Gideon Mack* by James Robertson

Question 22

 HINT Gideon suppresses his emotions at this point in the novel as he does throughout. The writer does not explicitly state how he feels but his actions show that he is going through different stages in dealing with Jenny's death.

At least three of:

- Gideon reflects on how strange it is to get into a car, which could be involved in a fatal crash (1)
- Gideon lashes out at John (1)
- Gideon wants to see evidence of the crash (1)
- He says that he is busy, shutting out Elsie (1)
- When alone with Elsie, he cries (1)

Question 23

 HINT   State the atmosphere clearly as part of your answer. You will get one mark for correctly saying what the atmosphere is.

Atmosphere - tense, uncomfortable (1)

AND one of:

- 'hardly spoke' (1) – tense, uncomfortable atmosphere, neither man knows what to say (1)
- 'She looked very beautiful' (1) – John attempts to comfort Gideon (1)
- 'Fine words…' (1) – Gideon reacts impatiently, does not want to be comforted (1)
- 'I'm sorry' (1) – John still feels need to apologise, just wants to make Gideon feel better (1)

Question 24

 HINT   There are several possible answers here; make sure you pick those that you are confident you can analyse in most detail.

Two of:

- 'We had gone one way, and drove back the other' (1) – statement, factual tone, lack of emotion (1)
- 'We were halfway through…before I realised where we were' (1) – suggests Gideon has completely switched off, is unaware of his surroundings (1)
- 'It was here somewhere.' (1) – use of the word 'it', not naming the accident or his wife's death (1)
- 'Had it been here?' (1) – inquisitive, wants to know the facts about the accident (1)
- 'Nothing was different. Everything had changed' (1) – antithesis emphasising that his life has been transformed but the world seems indifferent (1)
- 'My father's voice thudded against the inside of my forehead' (1) – Gideon is keeping his emotions in, feeling pain (1)
- 'I stared into the darkness' (1) – Gideon is confronting despair (1)
- 'was a part of her wandering out there somewhere?' (1) – thoughts of the supernatural (1)
- 'I felt like getting out' (1) – wants to escape (1)
- 'I said nothing' (1) – suppresses emotions, urges (1)

Question 25

One of:

- 'as if no one had lived there for years' (1) – feeling that he no longer belongs, his previous life has been erased (1)
- 'I've got things to do' (1) – wants to keep busy, does not want to confront reality (1)
- 'Let them sleep' (1) – imperative sentence, desire to take charge (1)
- 'in a gangster movie' (1) – feels he is doing something forbidden, inability to face up to the reality (1)
- 'children lost in the forest' (1) – feels small and vulnerable (1)
- 'in the middle of a horrible fairy tale' (1) – everything seems unreal (1)

Question 26

You might refer to some of the following in your answer. However, there are other possibilities that you could discuss.

- This incident is a turning point for Gideon and prompts the actions later in the novel.
- His relationship with his wife, Jenny, is complex. He seems to fall into a relationship and marriage with her almost by accident. She helps to convince him to become a minister. He does not choose his partner or his career out of passion or love.
- His shared grief with Elsie leads to them sleeping together.
- He has a close relationship with Catherine Craigie, an atheist who he is more open and honest with than anyone else.
- Gideon rejects the advances of his fellow minister, Lorna, and it is while walking with her that he falls into the Black Jaws.
- Gideon also has a troubled relationship with his mother, who is in a care home suffering from dementia. Gideon cannot connect with her, saying 'I could do nothing for her physically, emotionally or spiritually' but this distance between them stretches back to Gideon's childhood.
- As in other areas of his life, Gideon's relationships with women are full of self-deception, moral dilemmas, suppressed passion and confused emotions.

Prose, Text 4: *Kidnapped* by Robert Louis Stevenson

Question 27

> **HINT**   The phrase 'at least' should give you a clue here. It is a good idea to write four key points, as insurance.

At least three of:

- David looks at the house of Shaws and is disappointed by it (1)
- David decides he wants to go in for shelter and something to eat (1)
- At first the inhabitant of the house seems to be hiding (1)
- Then he (Ebenezer Balfour) threatens David with a shotgun (1)
- David persists and tells Ebenezer his name (1)
- Ebenezer relents and says that he will let him in (1)

Question 28

 HINT The key word in this question is 'contrast'. Make sure that your answer makes clear what the house of Shaws is like and how this differs from the land around. Both sides should be supported by quotation.

Surroundings

One of:

- 'The more I looked, the pleasanter that country-side appeared' (1) – David pauses to take in the scenery, and is increasingly impressed (1)
- 'all set…fields dotted…fine flight…' (1) – series of semi-colons allowing Stevenson to expand upon the abundance all around (1)
- 'hawthorn bushes full of flowers' (1) – beauty, plenty, lush (1)
- 'fine flight' (1) – alliteration emphasising the flock of birds (1)
- 'a kind soil and climate' (1) – personification, welcoming (1)

House

One of:

- 'barrack' (1) – suggest a military compound, fortress (1)
- 'went sore against my fancy' (1) – David is put off by its appearance (1)
- Contrast between extensive, detailed description of surroundings (1) and abrupt, emotional response to the house itself (1)

Question 29

 HINT You must clearly state what the mood or atmosphere is. If you can't work it out straight away look at the language used and then summarise the atmosphere at the end of your answer.

Mood – tension, suspense (1)

Writer's use of language (one of):

- 'The nearer…the drearier…' (1) – balanced construction, David's concern grows steadily (1)
- 'What should have been…' (1) – growing sense that the house is not quite right (1)
- 'bats flew in and out like doves…' (1) – bats are associated with mystery and evil, contrasted with doves, a symbol of peace (1)
- 'Was this the palace…?' (1) – questions, showing David's growing uncertainty (1)
- 'no sound…not a dog barked' (1) – eerie silence (1)
- 'lifted my hand with a faint heart' (1) – David is increasingly afraid (1)
- 'a dead silence' (1) – quiet, idea of death (1)
- 'clock inside…slowly counted the seconds' (1) – seems to be counting down, creating suspense (1)

Question 30

One of:

- 'It's loaded' (1) – blunt, threatening (1)
- 'be off with ye' (1) – dismissive, unfriendly (1)
- 'sharply' (1) – abrupt, harsh (1)
- 'defiantly' (1) – rude, cruel (1)

Question 31

You might refer to some of the following in your answer. However, there are other possibilities that you could discuss.

- Previous to this extract, David is extremely naïve, having been brought up in a comforting environment.
- However, it is clear even here that David is seeking adventure, 'Was it within these walls that I was to seek new friends and begin great fortunes?'
- His gullibility allows him to be kidnapped.
- However, the bravery and resolve, which here sees him face down a loaded blunderbuss, wins him the friendship of Alan Breck.
- Loyalty is a constant: David is loyal to Alan Breck and he expects the same in return.
- But David also grows up in the novel as his adventures test him.
- Throughout the novel he shows his flaws – pettiness, narrow-mindedness – and his qualities of bravery and loyalty.

Prose, Text 5: *The Cone-Gatherers* by Robin Jenkins

Question 32

At least three of:

- Neil and Calum begin to make themselves at home in the beach hut (1)
- Lady Runcie-Campbell, Sheila and Roderick come in for shelter (1)
- Lady Runcie-Campbell gets angry at Neil and Calum for using the hut (1)
- Neil and Calum leave (1)
- Lady Runcie-Campbell and Sheila express their disapproval of the cone-gatherers' behaviour (1)
- Roderick becomes upset (1)

Question 33

> **HINT**   You will be given credit for an appropriate quote. However, you must make a detailed comment too.

Relationship is close, loving, caring (1)

AND one of:

- Neil takes charge (1), 'Get your jacket off' (1)
- Calum craves Neil's approval (1), 'Is it a good pipe, Neil?' (1)

- Good-natured humour (1), 'It must have cost you a fortune.' (1)
- Calum teases Neil (1), 'I'm not telling' (1)

Question 34

Two of:

- 'a dog's bark, and voices' (1) – climax of paragraph emphasised by colon, disturbing peaceful mood (1)
- 'a scratching on it as of paws, and whining' (1) – onomatopoeia, mystery of what is outside, desperately trying to get inside (1)
- 'the loudest peal of thunder' (1) – noise, foreshadowing danger and disaster (1)
- 'her voice…was far more appalling to the two men than any thunder' (1) – Neil and Calum are terrified, Lady Runcie-Campbell is more frightening than the storm (1)
- 'silent abjectness' (1) – Neil is speechless with fear (1)
- 'he wished that the pain was twenty times greater' (1) – Neil feels ashamed of Calum, feels that he deserves to be punished for this (1)
- 'A lifetime of frightened submissiveness held it down' (1) – Neil feels intimidated and inferior (1)
- 'You'll hear more about this' (1) – threat from Lady Runcie-Campbell showing that this incident will have repercussions (1)

Question 35

 HINT Set out your answer clearly to show that you have covered the reaction of Roderick and how the writer shows this. This will help you when you check your answers and, even more importantly, will help the marker to see that you have covered both aspects of the question.

Reaction: upset, sulks (1)

Writer's use of language (one of):

- 'the corner to which he had retreated' – hides away (1)
- 'his own face grave and tense' – saddened, troubled (1)
- 'miserable' – unhappy, empathises with cone-gatherers (1)
- 'He did not move'/'He turned and pressed his brow against the window' – refuses to respond to his mother (1)

Question 36

 HINT It is important to have a clear understanding of the role that minor characters play in conveying themes and developing the plots of novels. Make sure that in your revision you do not focus solely on the central characters.

You might refer to some of the following in your answer. However, there are other possibilities that you could discuss.

- In *The Cone-Gatherers*, the characters all have symbolic significance.
- Roderick represents innocence, kindness and hope for the future. He is keen to learn and is fascinated by the world around him.

- However, his physical weakness suggests the fragility of this hope. He is described as 'weak in body and complicated in mind'.
- Roderick is quick to recognise the evil in Duror.
- He is capable of empathising with the cone-gatherers despite the class barrier between them. Unlike his mother and sister he believes that everyone should be treated equally.
- This is shown when he tries to convince his mother to give Neil and Calum a lift and he tries to convince his mother that they 'treat them unfairly'.
- The brothers are described as 'Roderick's heroes' and Roderick seeks to emulate Calum when he climbs the tree at the end of the novel.
- When he becomes stuck, Neil refuses to help as revenge for the injustice of his treatment by Lady Runcie-Campbell. Calum does help and this leads to the tragic conclusion.

Prose, Text 9: *Originally* by Carol Ann Duffy

Question 37

Two of:

- 'We…our…we…' (1) – pronouns suggest shared experience of family (1)
- 'a red room' (1) – uncertainty, lack of understanding, child does not know how to explain their method of travel which may be a car or a train carriage (1)
- 'fell through the fields' (1) – things happening quickly/out of control (1)
- 'singing our father's name' (1) – ambiguity about where the father is (1)
- 'cried…bawling Home' (1) – trauma (1)
- 'the city…the vacant rooms' (1) – thoughts returning to the home that they have left behind (1)
- 'blind toy' (1) – like the toy, the child is 'blind', with no knowledge of what lies ahead (1)

Question 38 (a)

 HINT   This question is an 'in your own words' question. Often these questions may come first, but be prepared for these types of questions elsewhere.

Two of:

- Growing up (1)
- Getting lost (1)
- Her voice sounding different to other people (1)
- The older children's behaviour (1)
- Not understanding the (swear) words other children use (1)
- Missing her native country (1)

Question 38 (b)

One of:

- 'All childhood is an emigration' (1) – metaphor suggesting that growing up is a journey to somewhere unfamiliar (1)

- 'up an avenue where no one you know stays' (1) – feeling of being lost and not belonging (1)

- 'unimagined' (1) – uncertainty, confusion (1)

- 'big boys eating worms' (1) – disgust, revulsion (1)

- 'like a loose tooth' (1) – irritation, nagging pain (1)

Question 39

> For full marks in this question you should choose at least two quotes and analyse both of them in detail.

Two of:

- 'But' (1) – conjunction suggesting a contradiction (1)

- 'forget, or don't recall' (1) – losing something, same idea repeated suggesting continued, failed attempts to remember (1)

- 'skelf' (1) – use of Scots word, suggesting that the language is becoming more familiar (1)

- 'skelf of shame' (1) – painful feeling of embarrassment (1)

- 'shedding its skin like a snake' (1) – an old life is left behind and a new one begins (1)

- 'just like the rest' (1) – the persona now belongs (1)

- 'Do I...?' (1) – question, uncertainty (1)

- 'river, culture…right place' (1) – list of all the things that she has lost (1)

- 'I hesitate' (1) – pause, showing the persona's doubts (1)

Question 40

You might refer to some of the following in your answer. However, there are other possibilities that you could discuss.

- Like *War Photographer*, this poem depicts someone who has conflicting emotions.

- In *Originally*, the persona wants to integrate but is also very conscious of what she has lost and feels her memories slipping away.

- In *War Photographer*, the photographer treats his work professionally but is plagued by traumatic memories.

- They also have a similar structure – 24 lines that can be split into three sections of eight, exploring different stages in the poet's exploration of themes.

- The theme of memory is also vital to *Havisham*, *Anne Hathaway* and *Mrs Midas*.

- Whereas the persona in *Originally* has no choice about leaving home, in the latter poem the persona must move on but also misses what she has left behind: 'I miss most, even now, his hands, his warm hands on my skin, his touch'.

Prose, Text 2: *Divorce* by Jackie Kay

Question 41

At least three of:

- Her mother has never said anything nice to her (1)
- Her mother has never been grateful for the household tasks she has carried out (1)
- Her father has bad breath (1)
- She dislikes the clichés used by her father (1)
- She thinks she would be cared for more in a home (1)
- She believes there are many parents who are better (1)
- Parents who do not raise their voices (1)
- Who are affectionate (1)
- Who are more cultured and refined (1)

Question 42

Two of:

- 'I did not promise' (1) – persona had no choice, wants to exert some independence/control (1)
- 'till death do us part' (1) – use of words used in marriage vows, promising lifelong commitment which persona is not willing to commit to (1)
- 'part I must, and quickly' (1) – unusual word order, emphasising need to escape (1)
- 'cannot suffer' (1) – suggests that she has endured enough (1)
- 'never, ever' (1) – certainty that this is a final decision (1)
- 'tedious chores' (1) – boredom, desire for change (1)
- 'your breath smells like a camel's' (1) – simile, exaggerating the disgusting smell (1)
- 'gives me the hump' (1) – comedy of comparison to camel, persona displaying temper (1)
- 'In this day and age?' (1) – question suggesting exasperation at the old-fashioned expression and attitude (1)
- 'I would be better off in an orphanage' (1) – persona completely rejects parents (1)

Question 43

They are perfect, ideal, wonderful (1)

AND one of:

- 'faces turn up to the light' (1) – positive associations, virtuous (1)
- 'who speak in the soft murmur of rivers' (1) – gentle, musical, connection to nature (1)
- 'who stroke their children's cheeks' (1) – affection, gentle (1)
- 'in the dead of night' (1) – dedication of parents, constantly caring for children (1)
- 'sing in the colourful voices of rainbows' (1) – musical, magical (1)

Question 44

One of:

- 'I never chose you' (1) – repeats earlier idea of having no choice about her parents (1)
- 'You are rough and wild' (1) – summarises the persona's criticism of her parents (1)
- 'that's not right' (1) – shows how judgemental the persona is (1)
- 'I will file for divorce in the morning at first light' (1) – decisive, shows future action, humorous (1)

Question 45

> **HINT** Using quotes will help you to write a good answer to the final question in the Scottish Texts section. There are many ways to help you remember quotes: write them on cue cards, sticky notes or a poster. But the best way is to revise them regularly and often.

You might refer to some of the following in your answer. However, there are other possibilities that you could discuss.

- The poem deals with strained family relationships.
- An interesting contrast would be with the persona in *Keeping Orchids* who wants to preserve the orchids her mother gave her to form a connection and prevent her memory from 'fading fast'.
- There is a strained mother-daughter relationship in *Lucozade* but towards the end the persona feels her mother is 'beautiful'.
- *Bed* is told from the point of view of a mother. Interestingly, the mother is plagued by her inability to express how grateful she is for the 'things she has tae dae fir me'. The seemingly selfless daughter in *Bed* contrasts with the petulant daughter of *Divorce*.
- Of course, these poems also have a quite different tone: *Divorce* is comical whereas *Bed* is contemplative and sad.
- *Gap Year* provides an interesting comparison with *Divorce*. The daughter in this poem, full of excitement about travelling the world, seems oblivious to her mother's feelings. She is caught up in the romance of Macchu Pichu and Costa Rica like the girl in *Divorce* creating an image of the ideal parents.

Prose, Text 3: *Aunt Julia* by Norman MacCaig

Question 46 (a)

At least two of:

- Gaelic is her first language (1)
- Speaks very quickly (1)
- Masculine (1)
- Connected to nature (1)
- Hard-working (1)
- Talented at weaving (1)

Question 46 (b)

One of:

- 'very loud and very fast'/'I could not…I could not…" (1) – repetition emphasising how incomprehensible the poet found Julia (1)
- 'men's boots when she wore any' (1) – unconcerned by appearance (1)
- 'stained with peat' (1) – close to nature (1)
- 'drew yarn marvellously' (1) – sense of wonder, magic (1)

Question 47

 HINT   The word 'develop' here means that you should pick up on some of the ideas already introduced and show how the poet expands on them.

Two of:

- 'crickets being friendly' (1) – the poet feels a sense of comfort, belonging (1)
- 'She was…she was…she was…' (1) – repetition, Julia is closely associated with her work and her surroundings (1)
- 'winds pouring wetly' (1) – alliteration (1)
- 'threepennybits in a teapot' (1) – thrifty, eccentric (1)

Question 48

HINT   Make sure your answer includes the **poet's feelings**.

Two of:

- 'Aunt Julia spoke Gaelic very loud and fast' (1) – return to idea of first lines, remembering her as if he was a child again, incomprehension (1)
- 'learned a little' (1) – attempt to get closer to Julia (1)
- 'By the time…she lay' (1) – regret that it was too late (1)
- 'silenced' (1) – the opportunity for communication is gone (1)
- 'But I hear her still' (1) – her memory lives on (1)
- 'welcoming me' (1) – still comforting and friendly (1)
- 'peatscrapes and lazybeds' (1) – returned to the land where she belonged (1)
- 'getting angry, getting angry' (1) – ambiguity of whether this line refers to the poet or Julia, frustration (1)
- 'so many questions unanswered' (1) – regret (1)

Question 49

You might refer to some of the following in your answer. However, there are other possibilities that you could discuss.

- This is an elegy, a poem to remember a loved one who has died.
- There are connections in both ideas and language to the other poems in the collection.

- At the end of the poem, Aunt Julia's voice is 'silenced.' Similarly, in *Sounds of the Day*, the 'clatter' and 'puff' of the opening lines ends with death: 'the end of all the sounds there are'.

- The mourning in *Memorial* also focuses on 'the silence of her dying,' but little comfort in the way memory forms a 'sad music'.

- These poems, including *Aunt Julia*, seem to offer little religious comfort in the face of death.

- *Visiting Hour* also presents a relationship where there is a distance between people, this time the 'distance of pain'.

- *Basking Shark* reflects on man's place in nature in a way that contrasts to *Aunt Julia*.

Prose, Text 4: *Winter* by Edwin Morgan

Question 50

Two of:

- 'The year goes' (1) – sense of ending (1)

- 'decay' (1) – decline (1)

- 'many a summer dies' (1) – personification, adds to mood of melancholy (1)

- 'The swan…a ghost' (1) – idea of death, haunting (1)

- Repetition of 'goes' (1) – loss (1)

- 'heavy light' (1) – seems oppressive, overpowering (1)

- 'swan-white ice' (1) – lack of colour (1)

- 'Even dearest blue's not there' (1) – without comfort or consolation (1)

Question 51

> **HINT**   When selecting a quote in poetry it is vital to choose a short phrase or expression. You will be rewarded for being selective and your analysis is also likely to be more focused.

Two of:

- 'stark scene' (1) – isolation, desolation, emphasised by sibilance creating hushed tone (1)

- 'warring air' (1) – conflict in nature (1)

- 'decay and break' (1) – word 'decay' repeated from first line, nature deteriorating, now strengthened by the destruction of the trees ('break') (1)

- 'the dark comes down' (1) – sinister atmosphere created (1)

- 'shouts run off into it and disappear' (1) – the human influence seems fleeting, mystery (1)

Question 52

> **HINT**   Make sure your answer includes both quotes and analysis.

- 'At last' (1) – a long time seems to have passed (1)

- 'lamps go too' (1) – light has gone, darkness is complete (1)

- 'fog' (1) – obscuring (1)

- 'drives' (1) – powerful (1)

- 'monstrous' (1) – terrifying (1)

- 'down the dual carriageway' (1) – overcomes human constructions (1)

- 'even in my room' (1) – the sense of loss has remained with the persona (1)

- 'grey dead pane' (1) – lack of colour, life (1)

- 'sees nothing and that nothing sees' (1) – repetition of nothing, emphasising bleakness (1)

Question 53

You might refer to some of the following in your answer. However, there are other possibilities that you could discuss.

- Like *Hyena*, this poem presents a harsh view of nature. In both poems the poet focuses on death and decay.

- The harsh winter described in this poem could be compared to the 'burnt out' plains of *Hyena*.

- *Slate*, too, describes tough weather – 'rains, blizzards' – but focuses more on what endures over time.

- The revellers in *Trio* triumph over the bleak winter with their good cheer: 'Monsters of the year go blank'.

- The bleakness of the final line – 'ice that sees nothing and that nothing sees' – recalls the similarly despairing final line of *In the Snack Bar*: 'Dear Christ, to be born for this!'

WORKED ANSWERS — Practice Exam C

Critical Reading, Section B: Critical Essay

DRAMA

1. There are many plays that would provide excellent material for this question. As with all critical essays structure is vital and there are a couple of things to keep in mind when structuring an answer to this question. It is vital to show the stages in the relationship: what it is like at the beginning; how it changes; what it is like at the end. Also, you need to make sure that you do not just focus on one character. For example, if writing about Macbeth it would not be enough so write about Macbeth's descent into evil; you must write about the way he stops seeking his wife's advice, the way she can no longer console him and finally, his reaction to her death. And of course, you must write about Lady Macbeth.

2. For this question, and all questions about drama, it is important to remember that you are writing about a play that was written to be performed. This should influence various things about your essay: using the word 'audience' instead of 'reader'; analysing the importance of stage directions, setting and lighting and referring to techniques such as dramatic irony. If possible, watch a stage version of the play. You may be able to buy one on DVD, find scenes you can watch online or even see one in performance. This will make a huge difference to your understanding and appreciation of the text.

> *HINT* If possible, watch a stage version of the play. You may be able to buy one on DVD, find scenes you can watch online or even see one in performance. This will make a huge difference to your understanding and appreciation of the text.

PROSE

3. A successful answer to this question will show how the mood or atmosphere develops. However, you must not slip into the trap of just retelling the plot. Make sure you write about the way that techniques such as setting and symbolism contribute to this atmosphere. Some novels, such as *The Strange Case of Dr Jekyll and Mr Hyde,* have a sinister mood throughout. In others, such as *Lord of the Flies*, there is a steady build-up of atmosphere.

 HINT   A really effective introduction does not just restate the question. It answers it clearly and specifically. The rest of the essay merely expands upon the points you make in the introduction.

4. The critical essay questions at National 5 are quite broad, to allow you to write about texts you have studied. However, you must take care not to slip into writing vague answers. In the very first sentence of your answer to this question you should specify the 'aspect of human nature' addressed by your text. Then, you should go into more detail about this in the rest of the essay. You should avoid just saying everything you know about the text. So, an effective first sentence might read something like this: *'The novel* Of Mice and Men, *by John Steinbeck, addresses the human need for companionship and the destructive power of loneliness.'*

POETRY

5. Poems that tell stories – narrative poems – can be an excellent option for study. They can help you to overcome preconceptions that sometimes put people off poetry. Border ballads such as *Kinmont Willie* and *Johnnie Armstrong* are full of murder, revenge and action. They also have a rhythm which can help you to remember key lines and quotes. There are also options such as *My Last Duchess* or more modern examples such as those written by Brian Turner about his experiences as a soldier serving in Iraq. To answer this question well you should provide a brief summary of the events of the poem. Then, you can go on to discuss the poem and its language in more detail.

 HINT   Keep any description of plot very brief. A simple retelling of the story will not impress the marker. However, if you can discuss the the significance of, for example, turning point or climax to the themes and ideas of the text, this will be rewarded.

6. This question provides a huge number of possibilities. The challenge for you is to make clear the 'message' of the poem in the introduction and in your analysis of the poet's language. The word 'message' means something different to 'theme'. The theme of *Dulce et Decorum Est* is war; the message is more specific: that people should not glorify war because it is devastating and traumatic. Make sure that you do not make vague statements about the poem; poetry is about trying to say something in a clear, concise way and your essay should reflect this.

FILM and TV DRAMA

7. The place where a film or TV drama is set can play a massive role in the mood, the plot and the portrayal of theme. For example, *Apollo 13* switches between two settings: the claustrophobic spacecraft and the NASA control centre. The use of these settings helps to sustain the tension and show the camaraderie of the astronauts. There are many thrillers and horror films where setting is used to create atmosphere. Another interesting option here would be *Broadchurch*, which depicted a seemingly idyllic seaside town torn apart by the murder of a child, revealing the dark secrets that societies keep hidden.

> **HINT**   Make sure that you discuss the influence of media techniques such as camera angle and lighting to show how the setting is depicted.

8. This question leaves it up to you why the sequence is important. Is it because of the development of character? Is it a turning point? Is it the climax of the film? You should be careful about what constitutes a 'sequence.' This is longer than a single scene but the scenes should be clearly connected. It may, for example, all be set in the same place.

LANGUAGE STUDY

9. Like many language questions, on the surface this seems quite simple. Many people will have reflected on the way that the way they talk is different to, say, their grandmother. However, a detailed answer would require clear examples and a grasp of whether they are differences in accent, vocabulary or syntax.

10. Looking at the way newspapers report upon, for example, football would highlight various areas for discussion. Tasks such as this are made easier by the availability of many newspapers for free online. Like all language questions a successful answer would have two things: examples of language used and a clear grasp of how to discuss these using the appropriate technical vocabulary.